# TEEN GIRL'S EMPOWERING JOURNEY: LIFE SKILLS FOR SUCCESS

AN INTERACTIVE GUIDE TO EMOTIONAL RESILIENCE, MONEY MANAGEMENT, CYBERSECURITY, AND BEYOND

TEEN LIFE LIT SERIES

THE GRAND SYNOPSIS PUBLICATIONS

# TABLE OF CONTENTS

*A Personal Prelude*    5

1. YOU'RE WORTH MORE THAN YOU KNOW    11
   Learning from the Greatest Poet    12
   Miraculous Synchrony of Cells, Neurons, and
   Heartbeats    14
   Self-Worth Is Nonnegotiable    14
   Master Your Self-Talk    16
   Self-Worth and Well-Being: A Dream Team    18
   Chapter Activities    20
   Lightbulb Moment    23

2. FROM SURVIVING TO THRIVING    25
   The Science Behind Puberty    26
   Managing Your Period    28
   Bra Shopping Guide    30
   Skincare 101    32
   Shaving    35
   Hair Care    37
   Nail Care    37
   Managing Unpleasant Odors    38
   Fitness Goals    39
   Ergo-Active Study Station    42
   Meal Mastery    44
   Chapter Activities    49
   Lightbulb Moment    52

3. THE ART OF AUTHENTIC SOULFUL LIVING    53
   Flourishing in Your Own Skin    54
   Chapter Activities    67
   Lightbulb Moment    68

4. NAVIGATING THE SOCIAL MAZE    69
   Breaking the Ice    70
   Dress Code    70
   Politeness    71
   Etiquette    72

Cultural Sensitivity 73
Body Language 73
Table Manners 74
Setting Boundaries 75
Navigating Peer Pressure 76
Toxic vs. Healthy Relationships 78
Cracking the Dating Code: Dos and Don'ts 79
Chapter Activities 83
Lightbulb Moment 84

5. FROM HURT TO HEALING 87
Understanding Bullying 88
Dealing with Bullies 89
Help, I've Been the Bully 90
Cyberbullying and Online Safety 91
Digital Footprint 93
Chapter Activities 94
Lightbulb Moment 95

6. TIME MANAGEMENT 97
What's Your Style? 99
Time Management Artistry 101
Time Mastery for a Healthier You 108
Time Management Roadblocks 113
Chapter Activities 114
Lightbulb Moment 116

7. MASTERING FINANCIAL LITERACY 119
Handling Personal Finances 121
Chapter Activities 131
Lightbulb Moment 132

8. DREAM, DISCOVER, DECIDE 133
Self-Reflect 134
Dream 135
Discover 137
Decide 138
Chapter Activities 140
Lightbulb Moment 142

9. NEUROPLASTICITY—REWIRING FOR SUCCESS 143
Chapter Activities 148
Lightbulb Moment 149

*Conclusion* 151
*References* 155

# A PERSONAL PRELUDE

## FROM THE MIDDLE EAST TO NORTH AMERICA

*Ugh, morning already? Hit snooze or face the day? Gotta drag myself out of bed after late-night Netflix. Now, what to wear? "Effortlessly cool" or "tried too hard"? Not into fashion statements, as long as it's not a cry for help. School's waiting—already running late. Algebra test today—great. Oh, that group project? Partners, please pull your weight this time.*

*Lunchtime is basically avoiding a cafeteria disaster—a game of finding the right table to avoid awkward stares. After the bell rings, it's a mad dash between extracurriculars, homework, and that constant buzzing of FOMO in the background. Friends? They're either my ride-or-die crew or a puzzle I'm still figuring out. Today's BFF could totally be tomorrow's stranger.*

*Then there's the late-night Instagram scroll, and everyone looks flawless. Do they really have it together, or is it just filters? Deep breaths—tomorrow's a new day, and who knows, maybe it won't be as crazy as today. Time to shut down the brain and hope for some decent sleep. How can I, though, with emotions all over the place, like, can we chill for a sec? Am I even doing it right? I swear everyone's got it figured out. But wait, maybe not.*

Been there, done that. We've all navigated these twists and turns, and it's okay not to have it all figured out. Ultimately, we're just trying to make it through the chaos with our sanity intact. But for me, growing up as a little girl under constant oppression, mornings were a whole different story.

Taking a moment to ponder what to wear? Nah. For twelve years, I had to deal with wearing the same ugly school uniform every day, all shades of gray that felt like wearing a huge cotton sack. Teamed with what we dubbed "family pants" because of their style, it was less about looking good and more about getting through the day without stumbling over that baggy mess.

FOMO? Nah, not really. With dancing, singing, or any kind of social club being forbidden, chilling at home was my thing. Outside was kind of meh, anyway. Not everyone felt that way, but openly expressing happiness in society felt almost like a crime. Risking it for a bit of teen excitement, like sneaking around or partying with rowdy crowds, wasn't my style. I liked keeping it low-key and avoiding drama.

I grew up in Iran—a place known for its breathtaking scenery but ruled by a regime that has never been big on letting people enjoy life, especially women. As the youngest of four siblings, I was born just before the Iran-Iraq war started. My early school days were chaotic, with bomb threats, hiding in underground hallways, and using stairs as shelters. Brainwashing, suppression, and oppression were common, especially for girls. Everyone had to follow the same rules and act the same way. While teens in other places were having sweet sixteen parties, I was getting in trouble for small things like grooming my eyebrows.

Toward the end of the war, I lost my dad, and my once-boring childhood quickly turned into an equally blah teenage phase filled with acne battles, wild hair, and a body I struggled to appreciate. My older siblings left Iran in search of a better life, leaving just my mom and me. Eventually, I also got the chance to leave, eager for a new beginning but feeling guilty about leaving my mom behind.

*The Azadi Tower (Freedom Tower), formerly referred to as the Shahyad Tower or "Shah's Memorial Tower," stands as a monument on Azadi Square in Tehran, Iran. [Chista, 2023. Artwork created using Midjourney].*

Growing up in chaos without learning essential life skills led to plenty of low points—struggles with confidence, awkwardness, and fear of not being "acceptable," let alone anxiety about not being "perfect." However, those low points, no matter how many there were, didn't define me, and they don't define you either.

Now, in the spirit of life's wild ride, I'm here to share the tough lessons I've learned over the years. Here's a quick overview of what you'll get from reading this book on mind and body recovery:

- **Embrace Your Uniqueness:** Beat self-doubt, nail your self-talk, and stay positive to celebrate your uniqueness.
- **Understand Puberty**: Get the lowdown on puberty science and learn to rock these changes with confidence.
- **Boost Your Confidence**: Change how you see things and embrace yourself.
- Handle Social Situations: From meeting new people to keeping friendships, learn the best ways to deal with social stuff.

- **Stand Up to Bullies**: Learn how to deal with bullies and take control of your life.
- Manage Time Better: Tackle time management issues and keep a healthy balance between work and life.
- **Handle Money Wisely**: Get savvy with your finances and nail those job interviews.
- **Find Your Passion**: Figure out what you love and what you're good at, and turn it into a career.
- **Unlock Your Potential**: Enhance your brainpower to be more adaptable, resilient, and creative for a brighter tomorrow.

This book has nine chapters. Each chapter has a main section, followed by activities that match what we've discussed. Use these activities not only to practice what each chapter teaches but also to get more ideas by sharing with friends or family for different viewpoints and learning.

We all face struggles, but remember, we're in this together. You're not alone, and it's totally fine not to have everything sorted out. Believe me—I'm still figuring things out too! This book is here to offer a fresh perspective on our shared challenges, drawing lessons from the bumps life has thrown my way—sometimes the hard way. Whether you connect with everything or just some bits, I'm sure you'll find wisdom in each lesson to apply to your life, now or down the road.

Continue to push through, just like many of us with tougher lives do. After all, undergoing immense pressure and hardship is what shapes diamonds into something truly remarkable. So take a breather, keep dreaming, keep learning, and always be your authentic self. You're doing better than you think, and remember, we've got this. Just focus on moving forward, taking life one wild day at a time!

Cheers to your journey,
Your Middle Eastern Bestie

*Chista, 2023. Artwork created using Midjourney.*

# YOU'RE WORTH MORE THAN
# YOU KNOW

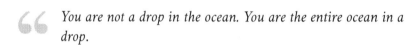

*You are not a drop in the ocean. You are the entire ocean in a drop.*

— RUMI

A while back, before I left my home country, my friends and I went on a trip to Dasht-e Lut, also known as the Lut Desert, to escape the city chaos. Situated in southeast Iran, it's called the hottest place on Earth and attracts astronomers and photographers from all over the world for its unique features (Kamkar, 2021).

Among Lut's surreal wonders, like the mesmerizing dune waves and the wind-carved Kaluts, the clear desert sky fascinated me the most. It was my first time seeing such a pristine, serene sky filled with twinkling stars like they were having a grand cosmic conversation. That's when a fellow traveler sparked a spiritual journey that I'm about to share, one that's been evolving ever since.

Have you ever looked up at the stars on a clear night and thought about how each galaxy, star, and planet is a masterpiece on its own? In such a vast space, you might feel small—just a tiny speck. But what if I told you that you're as magnificent as the universe itself? Yes, you, my friend, are "unique and magnificent." There you have it! I've shared what my insecurities kept me from believing for years.

*Chista, 2023. Artwork created using Midjourney.*

Let's explore together to understand your true worth. We'll dive into the wisdom of Rumi, a legendary poet whose words have touched hearts for centuries. We'll see what he says about self-worth and why you're exactly who you're meant to be.

## LEARNING FROM THE GREATEST POET

This chapter begins with Rumi's timeless poem, reminding us that each person is like a living artwork, reflecting the universe's divine essence. Just as the moon reflects the sun's light, your inner light can brighten up your life and those around you. Finding this reflection is a journey of self-discovery, where you let go of self-doubt to show your true colors. By looking within, you find your true worth and connection to the universe. Rumi's verses teach us that everything we need to succeed is already inside us. But how do we unlock this potential? It begins with self-discovery—digging deep to uncover our true selves without doubt or criticism holding us back.

*Do you know what you are? You are a manuscript of a divine letter. You are a mirror reflecting a noble face. This universe is not outside of you. Look inside yourself; everything that you want, you already have.*

— RUMI, *HUSH, DON'T SAY ANYTHING TO GOD: PASSIONATE POEMS OF RUMI*

Rumi says everyone's path is unique. Each person has a unique role in life, making the world more meaningful.

 *Do not be satisfied with the stories that come before you. Unfold your own myth.*

— RUMI

While he believes in humanity's greatness, he also acknowledges that life can be hard. He believes our challenges and imperfections don't define us as faulty beings but instead help us grow, start anew, and be nicer to ourselves.

 *Don't grieve. Anything you lose comes round in another form.*

— RUMI

Rumi's poetry encourages us to dig deep and recognize our ability to impact the world. We're all unique, bringing something special to the table. You're not just a small piece in a big, magnificent puzzle; you are a shining being, as impressive as the universe, capable of love and greatness. Seeing this helps you embrace your self-worth from a new angle.

## MIRACULOUS SYNCHRONY OF CELLS, NEURONS, AND HEARTBEATS

Ever wondered how you became you? It's this amazing mix of cells, neurons, and heartbeats that made you who you are.

The creation of a human is fascinating. Right from the start, genes, environment, experiences, and choices all come together to shape you. Genes act like your body's blueprint, and as you grow up, school and where you live also influence you.

For you to be you, it's like one miracle after another: a cell splits at just the right time, and your soul clicks into place with your body. Your body is like a masterpiece with incredible parts that keep you going. Your heart beats, your brain sends signals, and even your thoughts and dreams get in on the action. Every tiny cell counts, and they all join forces to make you, well, you. Your body tells a story of strength and resilience. That's why you're exactly who you're supposed to be—a masterpiece!

*Chista, 2023. Artwork created using Midjourney.*

## SELF-WORTH IS NONNEGOTIABLE

Ever tried something and totally failed? That's my story when I started working a month after arriving in the U.S. English felt like a puzzle, and my accent made me doubt every word. Even though I'd been learning English since middle school, my speaking confidence was rock bottom, making daily chats a real struggle. It went on until a coworker, amazed by my decent English after just a few years in the States, shattered my negative self-image. It hit me—I'd been too tough on myself, missing out on lots of chances for friendships and fun.

If you've ever doubted yourself, welcome to the club—it's called self-doubt, that pesky companion on the path to growth. It's that feeling that maybe you're not quite good enough or making the right choices. Self-doubt comes in different forms, from worrying about falling short to comparing yourself to others. It's like a sneaky road-block on your personal growth journey, holding you back from taking risks and trusting in your abilities. Positive self-talk boosts confidence, nudging you toward goals, while negative self-talk chips away at self-esteem, leaving you anxious. From my own experience of struggling with intermittent but brutally negative self-talk for years, I admit that mastering positive self-talk has been by far the most essential element for reaching a cool, confident vibe—believe me, it's a game-changer!

- **Boost Health**: Talking kindly to yourself isn't just about feeling good—it actually helps your health. It reduces stress, improves sleep, and boosts your immune system.
- **Build Confidence**: Believing in yourself is like giving yourself permission to shine and take charge.
- **Connect Better**: Positive self-talk isn't just about you; it helps you connect with others, improves communication, and builds trust.
- **Resilience**: Life's tough, but positive self-talk keeps you grounded when things get rough.
- **Stay Motivated**: Reaching goals isn't easy, but positive self-talk is your personal cheerleader, keeping you focused and motivated.

Overcoming self-doubt takes practice, but it's worth it for a healthier mindset. Let's dive in and learn how to kick that self-doubt to the curb!

## MASTER YOUR SELF-TALK

Our inner voice plays a big role in how we see the world. Let's chat about improving it for real-life perks!

- **Watch Your Thoughts**: First, pay attention to what's going on in your mind. Notice your thoughts during the day. When you catch negative self-talk, take a closer look to see what's causing it.
- **Deal with Negativity**: Check if those negative thoughts make sense. Remember, it's not about ignoring feelings but getting a clearer view. Here are some questions to help:

  - Are these thoughts based on facts or just guesses? Negative thoughts often rely on guesses rather than evidence.
  - Is this thought influenced by someone else's negativity or facts? Check if it aligns with reality or someone else's view.
  - Are you being fair or too hard on yourself? Consider if you're overly critical or aiming for perfection. Finding balance can make a big difference.
  - Do you see things as either perfect or a disaster? Real life is more like different shades of gray, not just black and white. Extreme words like "always" or "never" can cloud your thoughts.
  - Are you blowing things out of proportion? Recognizing exaggeration can bring things back into perspective.
  - What's the worst that could happen, and how likely is it? Often, the worst-case scenario is unlikely, which can ease unnecessary worry.
  - Did something similar turn out as bad as you're imagining now? If not, maybe your thoughts are exaggerated.
  - Put yourself in your friend's shoes. What advice would you offer yourself? This helps gain a balanced view.

○ Could there be another side to this situation? Exploring different viewpoints can provide a wider perspective. Talking with friends or seeking advice from a therapist could help.

- **Embrace Failure**: Feeling bummed about a flop? Let's face it: the more you try, the more chances you have of slipping up. If you can't handle setbacks, you might as well stay in bed! Embrace the idea that mistakes are crucial for growth. When you stumble, take a moment to reflect, learn from it, figure out how to improve next time, and see it as an opportunity to grow. Here are some ways to analyze your mistakes:

  ○ What could you have done differently?
  ○ How can you avoid the same problem in the future?
  ○ What tweaks or upgrades could help?
  ○ Any external factors to manage better?
  ○ Did you make the most of the available resources?
  ○ What lessons can you take away from this?

- **Tackle Your Flaws**: Do you feel embarrassed about losing your cool? Is being too emotional your weakness? Don't be ashamed of your imperfections! Recognizing your flaws is a sign of maturity, not weakness. Many adults struggle to admit when they're wrong, but by acknowledging your mistakes, you're taking a step toward improvement. Remember, nobody's perfect, and we all learn as we go.
- **Show Yourself Some Love**: Be kind to yourself. Would you speak to a friend that way? Treat yourself like you would a friend. You deserve it.
- **Highlight Your Strengths:** Focus on your strengths to always remember your worth and what you bring to the table. Embrace who you are, imperfections included, and understand that you're constantly evolving and working toward being your best self, step by step.

- ○ **Embrace Your Uniqueness**: Reflect on what makes you special. Ask loved ones what they admire about you.
- ○ **Discover Your Talents**: Think about what you're good at and enjoy. List hobbies or skills you excel in.
- ○ **Try Something New**: Explore activities that interest you. Learn skills that bring joy and excitement.
- ○ **Keep Learning**: Dive into books, articles, or workshops on topics that fascinate you. Stay curious and explore your interests.
- ○ **Set Goals**: Decide on achievable goals and break them down into steps.
- ○ **Celebrate Wins**: Recognize your achievements, big or small. Give yourself credit for your efforts.
- ○ **Challenge Yourself**: Take on tasks outside your comfort zone. See challenges as chances to grow, and don't let them intimidate you. Remember, failure is just another step toward success. After all, you wouldn't be running now if you hadn't fallen a few times while learning to walk!

- **Silence Your Inner Critic**: Ever wonder if those negative thoughts are just your inner critic talking nonsense? Recognize this sneaky voice, challenge its baseless claims, and watch it fade away. Remember, it's just a product of your mind.
- **Positive Affirmations**: Boost your mindset with positive affirmations. Short, upbeat statements can change your outlook by rewiring your subconscious and helping you adopt a more positive perspective.

## SELF-WORTH AND WELL-BEING: A DREAM TEAM

You might ask, "Does knowing my self-worth really make a difference in my daily life? Do I need to take responsibility?" Let's find out.

Think about how you treat something or someone special to you. Do you nurture it or let it fade away? Well, the same goes for self-worth. It's all about showing yourself some love and kindness, not being selfish. It's about giving yourself what you need to thrive, saying, "I know my worth, and I won't settle for less!"

Here's the scoop: Taking care of yourself isn't just about you. It's like a lively tune that adds joy and richness to everything you do. It boosts your inner cheerleader and earns admiration from others, inspiring them, too.

Think about your future self—what do you see? Someone stuck in regrets or living it up, embracing adventures, and cherishing every moment? Life's a one-time deal, so let's aim for the latter. It starts with believing "I deserve better" and refusing to settle for less. Listen to that inner voice because today's choices shape the amazing person you'll become tomorrow.

Self-worth and healthy habits are closely connected, shaping a life where you thrive, not just survive. Think of self-care routines as essential steps toward your best self—body, mind, and soul. These habits show how much you value yourself. But honestly, how much do you focus on self-care? With school, extracurriculars, and social activities, it's easy to feel like time is a luxury. But here's the truth: No miracle is coming to save the day! Graduating won't suddenly free up time; you'll probably just take on more responsibilities like work, family, and more. If you plan to have kids, remember that they'll learn from your actions, not just your words. If you don't prioritize self-care now, it will be even harder to fit it in later.

Time flies, and neglecting self-care can make us feel out of touch. We often ignore it, thinking it's selfish or unnecessary. But to do well in teenage life, you need to take care of your body and mind. After all, what's more important than living life to the fullest when we are here for it only once?

Wondering if self-care is your top priority? Here are signs you might be neglecting it:

- Eating meals in a rush without giving your body proper nourishment.
- Always on the go, never taking a break.
- Weekends blend with weekdays, leaving no time for relaxation.
- Sleep feels like a luxury.
- Exercise isn't a focus.
- Family time gets pushed aside.
- Mornings start with you already being tired.
- Your phone is the first and last thing you check daily.

If you neglect self-care, you could end up tired, stressed, and distant from loved ones, not to mention dealing with health issues. So, start prioritizing self-care now. Build healthy habits, prioritize your well-being, and boost your self-worth. Try journaling and hanging out with friends. This is just the beginning of your self-improvement journey—I'm laying the groundwork, and soon, it'll be all yours! Stick with it and watch yourself grow!

## CHAPTER ACTIVITIES

### Mirror-Mirror

Pause in front of a mirror. What do you notice? Is your inner critic in charge, or is your cheerleader taking the stage?

Recognizing your self-worth is crucial and encourages you to prioritize self-care. Share your feelings with friends to combat negativity and be open to constructive feedback.

- Respect yourself, acknowledge your flaws without doubting your worth, and quiet your inner critic.

- Stay realistic about areas for improvement and aim to do your best.
- Replace negative thoughts with positive affirmations to boost self-worth.

Inspire and share your findings with others; it helps on the journey to self-worth. Stay positive, and don't focus on the negatives. When your supporter outshines your critic, you're growing in self-worth.

### The Intrinsic Value Vault

Journaling offers many mental health benefits, particularly for self-awareness. Start a value vault by writing down the following:

- What you like about yourself, from quirks to talents
- Areas where you're growing with new knowledge and skills

When your inner critic chimes in, jot down your wins and goals and feel proud of your progress. Stay focused and driven, and keep moving forward. Turning negatives into positives is key to self-care.

Pay attention to this activity—it could greatly impact your career exploration. Hard skills are important, but remember to focus on your soft skills and personality traits, too. Don't worry; you've been developing these all your life, and they'll keep getting better.

**INFO BIT#1:** Scan the QR code to dive into an article on the top 120 skills for today's job market:

### *Your Future Canvas*

Create a calming ambiance with music, find a comfy spot, and imagine your future self—the woman you want to be. Evaluate your current actions and pinpoint your daily habits to shape that future. Write down your vision and break it into achievable steps. For instance, if you dream of running a business, focus on building self-discipline. I began reinforcing the mantra of "let's focus on what we need to do" instead of what we want to do at the age of four, as I believe it is never too early to start practicing discipline.

### *Poetry for the Soul*

Rumi turned his deep sadness into poetry after losing his friend Shams. His verses show his journey through grief, from shock to acceptance, and how creativity helps heal. In the end, Rumi found comfort in the idea that love goes beyond distance, uniting us all.

**INFO BIT#2:** Access tips for turning your voice into poetry using the QR code:

### *Self-Worth Insights*

Here's food for thought—no formal assignments, just a peek into diverse thinking. We looked at Rumi's ideas earlier; now, ponder these philosophies: Existentialism, Humanism, Romanticism, and Transcendentalism. Explore how they relate to your self-worth. It's not about right or wrong answers but discovering your unique perspective. Enjoy exploring!

LIGHTBULB MOMENT

In this chapter, we've been on a self-discovery trip led by Rumi's wisdom. He reminds us that we're all masterpieces, echoing the universe's essence. Rumi encourages us to see our flaws as chances to grow and refresh. By embracing our quirks and believing in ourselves, we can tackle doubts and build a sunny outlook. Always remember to embrace your worth, ignore others' opinions, and be kind to yourself. Gain respect, overcome negativity, and stay positive by pursuing goals and celebrating your strengths.

Next, we'll explore maturing and self-care practices for body and soul, even during tough times.

# FROM SURVIVING TO THRIVING

> *My mission in life is not merely to survive, but to thrive; and to do so with some passion, some compassion, some humor, and some style.*

— MAYA ANGELOU

As a kid, I thought growing up meant I'd have it all under control, but boy, was I wrong. Puberty hit me like a ton of bricks, especially with the whole acne ordeal. While everyone else seemed to breeze through it, I felt like I was barely keeping up!

If you're in the same boat, hang in there because you're not alone. Puberty shakes things up, inside and out, with acne, voice changes, and growth spurts grabbing all the attention. But there's more to it than meets the eye. It's like your personal Big Bang—a time of rapid growth and self-discovery.

In this chapter, you'll learn tips on how to handle these changes like a pro. Embrace this time with wonder and confidence, and appreciate your body as it transforms. Let's begin looking into these changes and some healthy habits to conquer this exciting phase!

## THE SCIENCE BEHIND PUBERTY

Puberty causes major physical changes in teen girls due to hormone shifts from the ovaries. Some of these changes include the following (Miller, 2019):

- **Growth Spurts**: Picture shooting up like a human rocket! Girls typically go through a growth spurt 6–12 months before their first period, gaining around 2–3 inches afterward, while boys usually hit it about two years later and hang onto it longer. So, if you're towering over most boys in your class right now, don't worry—it's common for girls to outgrow boys early.
- **Voice Changes**: Have you ever heard a boy's voice go from squeaky to deep in just a few months? A girl's voice can also change, though not as dramatically. Your voice might get slightly deeper or huskier as your vocal cords thicken during maturity.
- **Bust Development**: Time to address the elephant in the room —brace yourself for the likelihood of some bigger boobs. Whether they come all at once or gradually, every breast size is normal and unique. It's common for one to grow faster than the other, but don't sweat it—they'll even out eventually.
- **Hormones**: Get ready for a rollercoaster of hormonal changes! While they help you grow and mature, they can also bring mood swings and emotional ups and downs. Hang in there! With the right approach, you can manage them and keep your emotions in check.
- **Hair Everywhere**: Get ready to see hair pop up in new places like your pubic area and underarms. Some girls might even notice a bit of facial hair, but don't worry; we'll talk about solutions for that later on.
- **Pelvic Changes**: Your pelvic region may widen, a key change for future childbearing. But don't worry about having babies just yet.

- **Physical Strength**: Puberty will make you stronger, which might surprise you at first, but it's a serious confidence boost! You'll rock it in sports and physical activities like never before.
- **Body Temperature**: During this wild ride, your body temp might fluctuate. Blame it on the hormonal dance, especially during your menstrual cycle.
- **Metabolism Shift**: Your body's energy processing system is getting an upgrade. Notice any changes in hunger, energy, or weight? You're not alone.
- **Odor Changes**: Yep, your body's scent might switch things up too. No need to feel embarrassed—good hygiene is your best friend, especially during different cycle phases.
- **Brain Development**: Puberty isn't just about your body; your brain gets a major makeover, too. It's like a mental upgrade, with your decision-making part, the prefrontal cortex, going through some serious rewiring. This leads to new ways of thinking and emotional responses.

**INFO BIT#3:** Teens naturally take risks due to peer pressure and still-developing brains, which aren't fully mature until around age twenty-five (middleearthnj, 2014). This often leads to impulsive decisions and a sense of invincibility without considering the consequences. Not all risks are bad, though; some can help with personal growth, like stepping out of your comfort zone to try new things or face challenges. However, risky behaviors like substance abuse and violence can have serious consequences. Fortunately, with the right support and knowing when to seek help from supportive resources, teens can learn to distinguish between positive and negative risks and grow stronger through their experiences.

Now, let's find out how to handle these changes and help you thrive during this phase.

MANAGING YOUR PERIOD

Getting your first period can be a bit intimidating! It's when the uterus sheds its lining, which happens every 21 to 35 days. Periods vary in length and flow, starting as early as nine or ten for some and as late as fifteen or sixteen for others.

Historically, men were the record-keepers, so attitudes toward periods weren't the greatest. Medieval times were full of period shame, hiding periods, and seeing cramps as divine punishment. Pain relief was as basic as herbal remedies and, in some cases, as silly as burnt toad ashes. Early methods included wood tampons wrapped in lint and pads made of moss or buffalo skin (Team KT, 2018). So, count your blessings for being born in our era! Today, we have a plethora of products to choose from. The key is finding what works best for you. Let's dive into the options available!

- Pads

  - Flat, absorbent pads that stick to underwear, collecting menstrual blood
  - Available in various shapes and sizes
  - Pros: User-friendly and great for beginners

- Period Panties

  - Period underwear with a built-in absorbent layer for menstrual blood
  - Come in various styles and absorbencies
  - Pro: Comfy and leak-proof alternative to pads and tampons
  - Cons: Can be pricier initially due to reusability

- Tampons

  - Small absorbent plugs inserted into the vagina to collect menstrual blood
  - Come in various sizes and absorbencies
  - String for easy removal
  - Pro: Convenient, especially for sports or swimming
  - Cons: Learning curve

- Menstrual Cups

  - Cup-shaped devices made of medical-grade silicone or rubber inserted into the vagina
  - Can be worn for up to 12 hours
  - Pro: Environmentally friendly and cost-effective
  - Cons: Learning curve

- Period Disc

  - Similar to menstrual cups but flatter and sit lower in the vagina, resting on the cervix
  - Made of soft silicone and can be worn for up to 12 hours
  - Cons: Learning curve

- Pantiliners

  - Thin, absorbent pads for light menstrual flow or spotting.
  - Opt for high-quality, breathable products and change them regularly.
  - Smaller and less absorbent than regular pads, only suitable for light days or extra protection with tampons or menstrual cups.
  - Handy for the tail end of your period or for odor control.

Before your period arrives, have your preferred products ready and keep a backup kit nearby. Don't forget to explore pain relief options—while it may not sound thrilling, it's crucial. Remember, everyone's pain tolerance differs, so there is no need for comparisons. If discomfort strikes, speak up and try these tricks:

- **Over-the-Counter Pain Relievers**: Think ibuprofen or naproxen for menstrual cramps, but always follow the label's instructions. Taking them after a meal can protect your stomach.
- **Heat Therapy**: Apply a warm compress or heating pad to your lower abdomen or back for cramp relief.
- **Massage**: Gently massage your lower abdomen to ease cramps and tension.
- Essential Oils: Some oils, like lavender and peppermint, can work wonders. Dilute them and apply them to your lower abdomen or back.
- **Adequate Sleep**: Don't skimp on sleep—it reduces stress and boosts your mood, helping with cramp management.
- **Hydration**: Stay hydrated to ease bloating and constipation, which can worsen cramps.
- **Seek Medical Advice**: If cramps are severe or home remedies don't cut it, see your doctor for further options.

Remember, snug clothes might not be your best bet during your period. Opt for comfy, breathable outfits indoors, cover your back for kidney pain relief, and keep those feet cozy in socks. Loose pants can also help ease bloating. Comfort is key to easing period pain effectively.

## BRA SHOPPING GUIDE

Let's nail your bra fit! A great bra can make your day, but a bad one? Total headache. Many of us wrestle with bras that don't quite fit right —wrinkled cups, annoying underwires, or straps that won't stay put.

If you're on the hunt for your first bra, it's a mix of excitement and nerves. But don't stress—I've got your back!

*Chista, 2023. Artwork created using Midjourney.*

- **Know Your Size**: Grab a soft tape measure and wrap it snugly (but not too tight!) under your bust and round to the nearest even number for your band size. Then, measure around the fullest part of your bust. Subtract your band size from this number to find your cup size using a table. For example, if your band size is 34 inches and your bust size is 37 inches, you're likely a 34C.

| Bust Meas. (in) – Band Size (in) | 0 | 1 | 2 | 3 | 4 | 5 | 6 | 7 | 8 | 9 |
|---|---|---|---|---|---|---|---|---|---|---|
| Cup Size (US) | AA | A | B | C | D | DD | F | FF | G | GG |

- **Choose the Right Style**: Start with comfy options like sports bras or bralettes if you're new to bras. As you go along, try out different styles like demi, push-up, or balconette. Opt for soft, breathable fabrics like cotton or modal to keep comfy and steer clear of tight or scratchy materials.
- **Check the Fit**: Your bra band should hug your back comfortably, not too tight or loose. Adjust straps for a comfy fit without digging in, and ensure cups sit smoothly without overflow or gaps. If cups pucker, it's a no-go. Take a peek in the mirror to check if your breasts align between your shoulders and elbows. Opt for a bra that fits snugly on the outermost hook and prioritize comfort over trends.

- **Address Fitting Issues**

  - Slippery straps? Adjust them and keep an eye on them after washing. Consider trying a racerback style for ongoing problems.
  - Constantly adjusting straps to lift your bust? Maybe reconsider your band size.
  - Band riding up? Try a tighter hook or consider going up a band size while possibly downsizing a cup size—like trying a 36B if a 34C rides up.
  - To keep your bras in good shape, hand wash and air dry them to preserve the elastic.

- **Get Some Help**: Don't hesitate to ask a salesperson or bra fitter for assistance. They can help you find the perfect size and fit for your body.

## SKINCARE 101

Taking care of your skin during your teen years is crucial with all the changes going on. Forget the anti-aging craze at fifteen; stick to Skincare 101 instead (Khona, 2022).

*Chista, 2023. Artwork created using Midjourney.*

- **Product Type**: Go for oil-free and noncomedogenic products labeled "oil-free" or "noncomedogenic" for skincare, makeup, and sunscreen. Test for sensitive skin by applying a small amount for 7–10 days to check for reactions.

- **Gentle Cleansing**: Wash your face twice daily with a mild cleanser suited to your skin type. Use lukewarm water and gentle circular motions with your fingertips, and avoid rough tools like washcloths. Consider a cleanser with salicylic acid for oily or combo skin, and think about vitamin A or zinc supplements to cut down on oil and blackheads.
- **Serum**: Boost your skincare routine with a face serum for added hydration and nutrients. Apply after cleansing and toning but before moisturizing.
- **Moisturize**: Keep skin happy by moisturizing twice daily. Choose lightweight, oil-free options for oily skin, and skip fragranced ones if sensitive. Sunscreen-added products are a plus!
- **Sun Protection**: Make sunscreen a daily must, rain or shine! Apply broad-spectrum SPF 30 or higher, even under makeup, and reapply every few hours. Look for combo products to save time.
- **Exfoliate Weekly**: Keep your skin fresh with weekly exfoliation using gentle products or DIY mixes. Don't overdo it to avoid redness and sensitivity. A gentle exfoliating toner can give you a healthy glow.

Access an article with homemade face scrub tips by scanning the QR code :

- **Mask Up**: Treat your face to a mask session—it's like a spa day at home! Choose one that matches your skin type, but don't go overboard. Once a week does the trick without drying out your skin!
- **Makeup Etiquette**: Sharing isn't always caring, especially with eye and lip products. Keep an eye out for reactions; if it bugs

your skin, ditch it. Always remove your makeup before bed to prevent acne, even if it's labeled noncomedogenic. Feeling lazy? Opt for makeup remover wipes, but make sure they're gentle on those pores!

- **Lip and Hand Care**: Pamper your lips with lip balm before bed, and don't skip hand cream for dry hands!
- **Night Ritual**: Consistency is key in skincare! Take it easy; it's a marathon, not a sprint. Cleanse, moisturize, and use lip balm and hand cream before bed to let your skin recharge while sleeping.
- **Treat Acne**: Puberty breakouts are totally normal. Start with one acne product, and if it doesn't work in 4–6 weeks, add another. They target stuff like bacteria, clogged pores, and oil. If you've tried benzoyl peroxide, switch it up next time. Here's a quick guide (Palmer, 2024):

  - Benzoyl peroxide fights bacteria.
  - Retinoids, like adapalene gel, reduce oil and unclog pores.
  - Salicylic acid clears pores and reduces inflammation.

Pimple patches are small stickers that help treat pimples by drawing out impurities and reducing inflammation. They work fast to heal spots. If you're not sure how to handle acne or skin problems, chat with a dermatologist.

Here are some casual tips:

- **Hands Off**: Before diving into your skincare routine or makeup application, make sure to wash those hands. We're talking oil, dirt, and bacteria blockers here.
- **Keep It Gentle**: Resist the urge to touch or pick at your skin excessively, and go easy on the product overload. Popping pimples or experimenting with new acne treatments might seem like a good idea, but it can stir up trouble for your skin, causing even more breakouts.

- **Keep It Fresh**: Give your pillowcase and sheets a weekly wash to keep dirt and oil buildup at bay. By the end of the week, they're practically a haven for dead skin cells and bacteria just waiting to clog your pores and start a breakout party. If you've got oily hair or love your oily products, consider swapping them out more frequently.
- **Healthy Eating**: Treat your skin to a nourishing diet packed with veggies and fruits. Opt for good fats like salmon, avocados, and nuts over oily and sugary foods to keep your skin happy and glowing.
- **Drink Water**: Staying hydrated by drinking plenty of water keeps your skin healthy. Aim for eight glasses a day!

## SHAVING

Shaving is totally up to you—no age rule! Some girls start around eleven or twelve; others hold off. If you're going to shave, having a plan makes it go smoother. Check out some expert tips we've got!

- **Shower first**. Don't Skip! Shave in the shower after a few minutes of warm water to soften the hairs for an easier shave. Dry shaving can lead to razor burn, so steer clear of it.
- **Scrub to dodge ingrown hairs**. Regular exfoliation clears away dead skin and potential ingrowns, making for a smoother shave and fewer problems down the road.
- **Choose the right shaving cream or gel**. Go for non-foaming shaving cream or gel instead of foams; they give you a better barrier for a closer shave. No cream? Soap and lukewarm water do the trick too!
- **Pick the right razor and change blades often.** Begin with a single-blade razor if you're new to shaving; they're gentler on sensitive skin, boosting your confidence for your first shave. As you get better, switch to multi-blade razors for an even smoother shave. Keep changing blades regularly to steer clear of problems like razor burn and irritation.

- **Shave smart—get it right**. Hold the razor at a 30-degree angle, take short strokes, and rinse the blade after each one. Start shaving with the grain to lessen irritation, especially with longer hair. Later, go against the grain for a closer shave. Be cautious around the knees and ankles to dodge cuts. Underarm hair grows in various ways, so shaving in different directions can help. For the bikini area, go with whatever direction feels best for you.

  - Be ready for cuts by asking your folks for a styptic pencil. Dampen it and dab it on cuts or nicks to stop bleeding fast. You can also use a cloth to help stop bleeding by pressing it on the cut for a few minutes.

- **Stay hydrated—moisturize after shaving**. Use a soothing moisturizer after shaving to keep the skin soft and prevent ingrown hairs. Some girls like aftershave for sensitive skin—it stops ingrown hairs and leaves skin feeling fresh! Ingrown pubic hairs often clear up on their own, so wait a bit before treating them. If you've shaved, give it a few days before shaving again. You can also use a mild antiseptic on the ingrown hair to prevent infection.
- **Hair removal cream**. If shaving isn't your thing, hair removal cream is an option. It's pain-free, but hair grows back fast, and it might itch depending on your skin and the product.
- **Waxing**. Waxing gives longer-lasting hair removal, but it can hurt and be risky if not done right. Hot wax might burn and cause skin irritation, ingrown hairs, and redness. Some skincare products can even cause scarring with wax, so do your research before giving it a go!

## HAIR CARE

Hair care isn't just about cleanliness—it boosts confidence too! Check out these tips for keeping your hair healthy and looking fab (Teenology, 2021):

- **The Right Shampoo**: Pick shampoo and conditioner that match your hair type—oily hair needs oil control, while dry hair needs moisture.
- **Wash Regularly**: Cleanse your hair at least once a week, adjusting as needed based on your hair type and product use.
- Water Temperature: Skip hot water when washing your hair, as it can dry out and harm your locks.
- **Conditioner**: Smooth on conditioner to detangle and manage your hair; remember to use it after every wash.
- **Avoid Heat**: Heat tools can zap moisture from your hair; use a heat protectant if you must.
- **Watch Out for Chemicals**: Treatments like hair dyeing and perms can mess with both your hair and scalp. Maybe skip the DIY box dyes unless you're a total pro. Beware of products with sulfates and oils that can harm your hair and skin. Consider embracing your natural hair color or consulting a specialist for coloring tips.
- **Trim Regularly**: Regular trims help prevent split ends and keep your hair looking healthy!

## NAIL CARE

Here are some nail-care tips from the American Academy of Dermatology Association to add to your self-care routine:

- Keep your nails clean and dry to avoid infections.
- Trim fingernails straight across with slightly rounded corners for strength. For toenails, cut straight across to prevent ingrown nails.

- File nails in one direction to prevent breakage.
- Try using a nail strengthener.
- Leave cuticles alone; they're the nail's natural protectors, so no pushing or cutting!
- Keep your nails and cuticles moisturized.
- Avoid biting your nails.
- Steer clear of harsh chemicals like nail polish remover and bleach.
- Wear gloves for housework or gardening.

Toenails matter, too, even if they don't always get the spotlight. They need some TLC!

- Give your toes wiggle room in shoes to avoid ingrown toenails.
- Change socks daily for healthy feet.
- Rock flip-flops in public to dodge infections like athlete's foot.
- Keep an eye on your nails; if you see dark streaks or crumbling, visit a skin expert.

## MANAGING UNPLEASANT ODORS

As puberty hits, you might pick up some new scents. Glands under your arms and down there get busy, pumping out sweat and oils, which can lead to body odor. It's not just sweat; bacteria feasting on oily sweat causes the smell. Even feet can get a tad funky with trapped moisture. No stress; sweating is totally normal! Let's chat about how to handle these changes.

- **Freshen Up**: Shower daily and scrub your underarms to get rid of sweat and stinky bacteria. Consider using antibacterial soap for extra odor control.
- **Deo Time**: Use deodorant to cover up smells or antiperspirant to cut down on sweat with aluminum salts.

- **Choose Breathable Fabrics and Change Regularly**: Go for cotton, silk, or wool for better airflow. Wear moisture-wicking materials for workouts and switch out of sweaty clothes to avoid bacteria buildup.
- **Powder Power**: Use talcum powder to absorb moisture and reduce friction. Apply to feet and inner thighs after showering, but avoid it if you have asthma.
- **Mind Your Diet**: What you eat affects body odor; foods like onions and garlic can change how you smell. Cut back on caffeine and alcohol to sweat less.
- **Mouth Care**: Brush twice daily and floss regularly to keep bad breath away, which can help manage body odors.

Navigating the teenage years can be tricky, but don't worry. With these tips, you'll be sailing smoothly soon. Just remember, it's about discovering yourself, not chasing perfection.

## FITNESS GOALS

Studies prove that being active isn't just about staying fit—it's great for your mind, too! It helps keep you healthy and improves your mental well-being. Exercise boosts your memory, making it sharper with each workout and strengthening your brain over time.

### *Guidelines for the Active Teen*

The Physical Activity Guidelines for Americans suggest 60 minutes or more of moderate-to-vigorous activity daily for kids aged six to seventeen (Piercy, 2022). Let's break it down:

- → **Aerobic**: Get moving! Spend 60 minutes a day doing activities that get your heart pumping. Mix it up with moderate-to-intense aerobic exercises and go hard at least three days a week.

→ **Muscle-Strengthening**: Don't skip the muscle work! Make sure to do muscle-strengthening exercises at least three days a week—it's like throwing a party for your muscles!

→ **Bone-Strengthening**: Include bone-strengthening exercises in your routine at least three days a week to maintain bone strength. Keep your bones tough!

Here's a table breaking down what teenagers do based on how much energy they burn, following the Physical Activity Guidelines for Americans:

| Type of Physical Activity | Examples |
|---|---|
| Moderate–intensity aerobic | • Brisk walking<br>• Bicycle riding<br>• Active recreation, such as kayaking, hiking, or swimming<br>• Playing games that require catching and throwing, such as baseball and softball<br>• House and yard work, such as sweeping or pushing a lawn mower<br>• Some video games that include continuous movement |
| Vigorous–intensity Aerobic | • Running<br>• Bicycle riding<br>• Active games involving running and chasing, such as fag football<br>• Jumping rope<br>• Cross-country skiing<br>• Sports such as soccer, basketball, swimming, and tennis<br>• Martial arts<br>• Vigorous dancing |
| Muscle strengthening | • Games such as tug of war<br>• Resistance exercises using body weight, resistance bands, weight machines, and hand-held weights<br>• Some forms of yoga |
| Bone strengthening | • Jumping rope<br>• Running<br>• Sports that involve jumping or rapid change in direction |

*Special Tips*

• **Fitness and Disabilities**: If you've got physical limitations, team up with a health pro to craft a plan that suits you. If the ideal activity isn't doable, keep moving and dodge the stillness trap.

- **Size and Ability**: Adjust gym gear to your size to dodge discomfort and injuries. It's all about feeling great, not fitting into a mold.
- **Effort Trumps Performance**: Focus on honing skills and playing fair rather than just winning. That's the real victory that lasts.
- **Body Image**: Embrace strength and athleticism; they shine brighter than superficial standards.
- **Keep It Fun**: Pick activities you enjoy, like jumping rope, to keep fitness a lifelong passion.

### Your Sample Fitness Plan

Here's a quick fitness plan to kickstart your workout routine. Ease into it and gradually push yourself. Remember to warm up beforehand and cool down afterward to prevent any strains or stiffness!

- Time to get moving with your warm-up! It's not just about getting the blood flowing but also gearing up for the workout ahead. Try these dynamic stretches for 30–60 seconds each:

  - → **Arm Circles**: Swing those arms in circles to prep your joints.
  - → **Leg Swings**: Loosen up with side-to-side leg swings.
  - → **Lunge Walks with a Twist**: Combine lunges and twists for a full-body warm-up.
  - → **Walking Knees to Chest**: Bring your knees up as you walk in place.
  - → **Straight Leg Kicks**: Stretch those hamstrings with kicks.

- **Let's get this fitness fiesta started at home!** When the gym's too far away, go for a home bodyweight workout. Start easy and build up:

→ **Plank**: Hold for 15 seconds.
→ **Press-Up**: Three sets of 30 seconds.
→ **Sit-Ups**: Three sets of 30 seconds.
→ **Standing Squats**: Three sets of 30 seconds.
→ **Mountain Climbers**: Three sets of 30 seconds.
→ **Star Jumps**: Three sets of 30 seconds.
→ **Burpees**: Three sets of 30 seconds.

- **Your cool-down**. Post-workout, relax with these static stretches for 30 seconds to a minute each:

  → **Quadricep Stretch**: Pull one ankle toward your glutes for a quad stretch.
  → **Hamstring Stretch**: Reach for your toes to stretch those hamstrings.
  → **Standing Calf Stretch**: Lean on a wall and step one foot back for a calf stretch.
  → **Cobra Stretch**: Push up with your hands for a chest stretch.

Mix up your workouts with a variety of activities. Focus on skills and have fun. Your body will appreciate the change!

## ERGO-ACTIVE STUDY STATION

Alright, let's talk turkey: How you sit today shapes your well-being tomorrow. Poor posture can mess with your muscles, confidence, and energy levels. Time to perfect your sitting setup for productive, killer study sessions!

### *Ergo-Essentials*

- Keep your screen at eye level and arm's length to dodge slouching and save those peepers.

- Choose a mouse over a touchpad to keep your wrists comfortable.
- Keep your keyboard close to your belly, near the table edge, to cut down on arm movements.
- Grab a comfy office chair with armrests if you can swing it; make sure it's adjusted for knee room and grounded feet.
- A tilting desk is a top choice for neck comfort and lighting. Standing desks keep you standing tall and ease shoulder strain.
- Study in well-lit spaces to fend off eye strain and headaches.

**INFO BIT#4:** It's said that Johann Sebastian Bach, the famous composer, faced vision issues later in life, probably from things like cataracts. It seems spending lots of time composing in dark churches and burning the midnight oil didn't help his eyes much, so take the last note very seriously (Tarkkanen, 2013). Ensure there is enough lighting before reading!

### Posture Principles

- Sit up straight and find comfort in the chair.
- Add a pillow or cushion for extra back support.
- Rest your arms on the armrests comfortably.
- Keep feet flat on the floor, avoiding dangling legs.
- Follow the 90-90-90 rule for knees, hips, and elbows.
- Consider trying standing desks or stability ball chairs for a posture boost and variety.

### Rethink "Sit Still"

Sitting for hours while studying isn't great for your body or brain. Research shows that sitting for over eight hours daily without exercise is as risky as being obese or smoking. However, exercising for 60 to 75 minutes daily can help counter these effects. Taking breaks to move around boosts physical and mental well-being and learning.

Adding movement to study sessions, like cycling, improves memory without affecting brainpower (Fairbank, 2022). Moving keeps your brain active and focused, while a bit of discomfort can boost stamina and be a game-changer. Pushing past your comfort zone helps overcome fears and leads to growth. Try some quick, desk-friendly workouts while you study (Zabriskie and Heath, 2019)!

1. **Abdominal Lifts**: Try some upper-body workouts while studying torso organs. Cross your legs on the chair and lift your body, using your arms for support. It's a cool trick, almost like levitating!
2. **Ab Swivel**: Make your swivel chair work for you with the oblique swivel. Hold onto your desk and use your arms to twist back and forth about 15 times. Tone those abs and maximize your chair workout!
3. **Leg Planks**: Stuck studying? Try lifting your legs at a 90-degree angle for 10 seconds. It's an easy exercise you can do right from your desk!
4. **Chair Squats**: Fight sitting fatigue with chair squats. Stand up, squat halfway over your chair, hold for 10 seconds, and repeat 20 times.
5. **Water Bottle Curls**: Always carrying a water bottle? Try a quick workout by curling it to your shoulder around 15 times. It boosts wrist strength and is great for exams or any academic and professional tasks. Stay hydrated, multitask, and keep active!
6. **Under-the-Desk Bike**: For a lasting way to stay active while studying, think about getting an under-the-desk bike. It's a game-changer for adding physical activity to your study routine!

## MEAL MASTERY

Staying healthy is super important, and here's why: Think of your body as a high-performance car. You wouldn't put low-quality fuel in it, right? A healthy diet is like premium fuel, keeping you energized, focused, and in top shape. It's not just about fitness; it affects your energy, school performance, and long-term health. Eating right helps with growth, puberty, and even mood (John Hopkins Medicine, 2024). So, let's dive into what a balanced diet really means!

*Chista, 2023. Artwork created using Midjourney.*

### MyPlate Food Groups

MyPlate is a practical nutrition guide from the USDA that highlights five food groups: Fruits, Vegetables, Grains, Protein Foods, and Dairy. The key is to mix it up within each group and aim for variety.

- Fill half your plate with fruits and veggies.
- Choose whole grains and vary your protein sources.
- Opt for low-fat or fat-free dairy or lactose-free or fortified soy options.

MyPlate guides you toward your self-care goals—one habit at a time.

**INFO BIT#5:** Want to boost your food knowledge and become a foodologist? Scan the QR code below for more information on nutrients. You might just inspire and change lives!

*Main Principles of Holistic Meal Practices*

Is a healthy diet just about what's on our plate? Good food choices are key, but timing and how we eat also make a big difference. Discover some essential holistic meal practices to boost your health!

- **Perfect Timing**: Eat bigger meals earlier in the day for better digestion and sleep. Stick to a regular breakfast, lunch, and dinner to keep your energy up.
- **Mindful Eating**: Slow down and savor each bite without distractions. Turn mealtime into a mini-culinary adventure.
- **Portion Control Is Key:** No need to break out the measuring tape. Use a smaller plate to keep portions in check. Skip the carb overload, and maybe try measuring cups if you're feeling fancy. Meal prepping can help you stay on track.
- **20-Minute Timeout**: Before round two, give it 20 minutes. Your stomach needs time to hit the *full* button. Take a chill pill and see if you're still hungry.
- **Snack Smart**: Opt for nutrient-packed snacks like nuts or fruit but watch those portions.
- **Feelings vs. Hunger**: Keep it real with yourself. Know if you're truly hungry or just riding the emotional wave. I realized I was hooked on nuts during study sessions to tame anxiety, which led me to gain some extra pounds! Identify your cravings and tackle them head-on.

- **Stay Hydrated**: Keep sipping water throughout the day and swap sugary drinks for herbal teas or infused water. Stay refreshed!

**INFO BIT#6:** Fruit-infused water is a tasty blend of your favorite fruits and herbs, such as lemon, lime, mint, or basil. This trend isn't new, even Renaissance folks flavored water with flowers! While fruit adds flavor, the water doesn't absorb many nutrients. Squeezing the fruit might increase the vitamins, but research is ongoing (Juber, 2022).

*Chista, 2023. Artwork created using Midjourney.*

### Sample Weekly Meal Plan

Let's get cooking! Planning meals can be tricky, even with good nutrition knowledge. Here are some food ideas to kickstart your healthy eating journey—grab your measuring cups and apron, girl!

| Day | Breakfast | Snack | Lunch | Snack | Dinner |
|-----|-----------|-------|-------|-------|--------|
| 1 | 1 cup oatmeal with 1/2 cup sliced strawberries 1 boiled egg 1 cup low-fat milk | 1 medium apple | Grilled chicken salad with mixed greens, cherry tomatoes, cucumbers, and 2 tablespoons of olive oil vinaigrette dressing 1 cup steamed broccoli | 1/4 cup almonds | Baked salmon with quinoa 1 cup roasted sweet potatoes 1 cup sautéed spinach |

| | | | | | |
|---|---|---|---|---|---|
| 2 | Greek yogurt parfait with 1 cup yogurt, 1/2 cup granola, and 1/2 cup mixed berries 1 slice whole-grain toast with 1 tablespoon almond butter | 1 medium orange | Whole-grain wrap with turkey, lettuce, tomatoes, and a side of sliced bell peppers 1 cup mixed vegetables stir-fried in olive oil | 1/2 cup hummus with carrot sticks | Quinoa-stuffed bell peppers Grilled zucchini and yellow squash 1 cup sliced watermelon |
| 3 | 2 whole-grain waffles with 1/2 cup mixed berries 1 cup low-fat milk | 1 medium banana | Lentil soup with a side of whole-grain roll 1 cup mixed greens salad with balsamic vinaigrette | 1/4 cup walnuts | Baked chicken breast with brown rice 1 cup steamed asparagus 1 medium peach |
| 4 | Scrambled eggs with spinach and feta cheese 1 slice whole-grain toast | 1 cup mixed berries | Quinoa salad with chickpeas, cherry tomatoes, cucumbers, and a lemon-tahini dressing 1 cup sliced bell peppers | 1/2 cup cottage cheese with pineapple chunks | Shrimp stir-fry with mixed vegetables and brown rice 1 cup roasted Brussels sprouts |
| 5 | Smoothie with 1 cup spinach, 1/2 banana, 1/2 cup Greek yogurt, and 1 tablespoon chia seeds | 1 medium apple | Turkey and avocado wrap with whole-grain tortilla 1 cup steamed broccoli | 1/4 cup almonds | Grilled tilapia with quinoa 1 cup roasted sweet potatoes 1 cup sautéed spinach |
| 6 | Whole-grain English muffin with scrambled eggs, tomato slices, and 1 slice of low-fat cheese | 1 medium orange | Chickpea salad with mixed greens, cherry tomatoes, cucumbers, and a light vinaigrette dressing 1 cup mixed vegetables stir-fried in olive oil | 1/2 cup hummus with carrot sticks | Baked salmon with quinoa 1 cup roasted Brussels sprouts 1 medium peach |
| 7 | Greek yogurt parfait with 1 cup yogurt, 1/2 cup granola, and 1/2 cup mixed berries 1 slice whole-grain toast with 1 tablespoon almond butter | 1 medium banana | Lentil soup with a side of whole-grain roll 1 cup mixed greens salad with balsamic vinaigrette | 1/4 cup walnuts | Baked chicken breast with brown rice 1 cup steamed asparagus 1 cup sliced watermelon |

This meal plan is just a starting point; adjust it to fit your tastes and needs. Explore a variety of food groups, incorporate antioxidants like dark chocolate and healthy oils, and experiment with different cuisines to savor the diverse offerings from our planet and the various cultures it houses! The goal is to help you cultivate healthy eating habits that will not only benefit you but also your present and future family for years to come!

## CHAPTER ACTIVITIES

### *The Self-Care Guru Quiz*

Feel free to answer these questions honestly. Pick the option that fits your situation best for each question.

1. I prioritize getting enough sleep most nights.

    a) Almost never          c) Usually
    b) Sometimes           d) Almost always

2. I make time for regular physical activity that I enjoy.

    a) Almost never          c) Usually
    b) Sometimes           d) Almost always

3. I eat nutritious and balanced meals most days of the week.

    a) Almost never          c) Usually
    b) Sometimes           d) Almost always

4. I engage in activities that bring me joy and relaxation on a regular basis.

    a) Almost never          c) Usually
    b) Sometimes           d) Almost always

5. I practice healthy coping mechanisms for stress and difficult emotions.

    a) Almost never            c) Usually
    b) Sometimes            d) Almost always

6. I maintain healthy relationships with friends and family members.

    a) Almost never            c) Usually
    b) Sometimes            d) Almost always

7. I set realistic goals for myself and work toward achieving them.

    a) Almost never            c) Usually
    b) Sometimes            d) Almost always

8. I take time for self-reflection and personal growth.

    a) Almost never            c) Usually
    b) Sometimes            d) Almost always

9. I prioritize my well-being and seek help when needed.

    a) Almost never            c) Usually
    b) Sometimes            d) Almost always

10. I feel generally satisfied with my overall self-care practices.

    a) Almost never            c) Usually
    b) Sometimes            d) Almost always

**Scoring:** Give yourself one point for each "Almost always" or "Usually" response, two points for each "Sometimes" response, and three points for each "Almost never" response. Tally your points and compare them to the total score results below:

- 0–10 points: High level of self-care
- 11–20 points: Moderate level of self-care
- 21–30 points: Low level of self-care

This quiz will give you a quick snapshot of your self-care habits, allowing you to see if you're on point or could use some improvement.

### Your Personalized Freshness Kit

Let's put together your personalized freshness kit! Gather with friends to brainstorm must-haves that keep you feeling fresh and confident. After sharing ideas, refer to the flipped list of answers below to compare and reflect.

Deodorant  Antiperspirant  Wet Wipes  Tissues  Pocket-Sized Perfume

Body Mist  Travel-Sized Toothbrush and Toothpaste  Breath Fresheners  Hand Cream

Hairbrush or Comb  Hair Ties or Clips  Lip Balm  Mini Facial Cleanser  Hand Sanitizer

Mini Moisturizer  Travel-sized menstrual products or panty liners  Reusable Water Bottle

Travel-Sized Sunscreen  Nail Kit  Travel Mirror  Emergency Stain Remover Pen

Earbuds  Headphones  Travel-Sized Dry Shampoo  Disposable Face Masks  Book

Hydrating Face Mist  Compact Pouch or Cosmetic Bag  Phone Charger

Epinephrine Auto-Injector (in case of severe allergies or anaphylactic reactions)

Rescue Inhaler (if you are Asthmatic)  Over-the-counter Pain Relievers

Motion Sickness Medication  Anti-Diarrheal Medication  Medical Information Card

Compact First Aid Kit  Mini Sewing Kit  Dental Floss or Picks  Mini Umbrella

Emergency Snacks  Mini Flashlight  Emergency Contact Card  Self-defense tool

Mini Notepad and Pen  Portable Fan  Reusable Shopping Bag  Small Trash Bag

### DIY Face Mask Extravaganza

Join us for a glow-up session and create refreshing face masks using honey, yogurt, avocados, and more! While the masks do their magic, craft your own infused water blends to keep the vibes high. Hydrate with your creations and elevate your skincare game with style—it's an evening of relaxation, creativity, and radiant vibes!

## LIGHTBULB MOMENT

We covered puberty's quirks to help you be more prepared. Remember, your body is yours to nurture for a brighter future.

Next up, let's explore essential mental skills—think of them as hiking boots for navigating your teen years. These skills will guide you through adolescence and beyond!

# THE ART OF AUTHENTIC SOULFUL LIVING

> *Slow, soulful living is all about coming back to your truth, the only guidance you'll ever need. When you rush, you have the tendency to follow others. When you bring in mindfulness, you have the power to align with yourself.*
>
> — KRIS FRANKEN

Ever heard of living a soulful life? It's about syncing your actions with your deepest values, finding joy in the little things, and leaving a positive mark. It's being genuine, purposeful, and feeling connected to something greater. Simply put, it's about being yourself and finding happiness. Sounds amazing, doesn't it? But I get it; it's tough to picture when you're overwhelmed and feeling down.

Let's look at what a meaningful life means in different cultures. Ancient Egyptians followed "Ma'at," focusing on truth, balance, and morality. Ancient Greeks sought purpose through philosophy, intellect, and ethics. During the Renaissance, humanism encouraged people to pursue knowledge and self-improvement for the benefit of all. Samurai followed Bushido, valuing loyalty, honor, and self-discipline. Native Americans celebrated their heritage through powwows, strengthening community and ancestral ties. Confucian teachings in China emphasized virtue, family respect, and inner harmony. In India, "Dharma" guides moral duty and spiritual purpose. Aztecs honored gods and ancestors to maintain cosmic balance for community prosperity and happiness.

As we explore different cultures, we find a common desire for authentic living, connecting with others, and making a positive impact. These timeless ideas show us that true happiness comes from being genuine and making a difference. By learning from the past, we can create a path to a meaningful life filled with purpose, honesty, and happiness. In this chapter, we'll discuss the mindset for a fulfilling life, how to begin, and the skills you'll need. Ready to live your best life? Let's dive in!

*Chista, 2023. Artwork created using Midjourney.*

## FLOURISHING IN YOUR OWN SKIN

For the longest time, I felt insecure about my look. As I grew older, I learned some makeup tricks that helped me feel more like myself. However, even with a new look, my confidence still lagged. It took me a while to realize that true confidence comes from within. If you're not happy with yourself inside, no amount of makeup can fix that. Overcoming self-doubt and embracing who you are are the real secrets to feeling comfortable in your own skin.

*Health over Appearance*

Dealing with self-doubt often comes from putting looks before health. While society emphasizes appearance, understanding that true beauty comes from living a balanced, healthy life is key. Here's why focusing on health matters for personal growth:

- **Boosts Confidence**: Taking care of your health boosts your inner confidence and overall well-being.
- **Fuels a Growth Mindset**: Embracing a healthy lifestyle encourages a mindset of growth and continual improvement.
- **Flourish with Health**: Investing in your health boosts vitality and confidence, helping you thrive authentically.

Remember, prioritizing your health lays the groundwork for self-acceptance and success. If self-doubt lingers, Chapter 1 has insights to help shift your perspective.

*Self-Expression*

*Chista, 2023. Artwork created using Midjourney.*

Self-expression is all about sharing thoughts, feelings, and experiences —it's a big part of connecting with others and understanding the world. It's crucial for living a rich life because it helps us:

- **Connect with Others**: Sharing our thoughts deepens connections and helps others get us better.

- **Build Relationships**: Being open builds trust and closeness in relationships.
- Understand the World: Expressing ourselves helps us make sense of where we fit in.
- **Heal and Grow**: Self-expression can be like medicine, helping us heal and bringing our dreams to life.

Self-expression comes in many forms, and here are some favorites to try out:

- **Fashion**: Show your style with clothes, accessories, and colors. It's not just about appearance; it boosts confidence and lets you express moods and messages. Fashion is a fun way to be yourself and make a statement.
- **Art**: Art goes beyond words, giving a safe space to express feelings and bond with others. Making art turns thoughts into something real, promoting self-awareness. It's not just about pretty pictures; art gives new viewpoints, questioning norms, and understanding the world.
- **Music**: Music is a fantastic way to express yourself, bringing people together with universal vibes and emotions. Whether making or listening to music, it reveals personal tastes and aspirations, uniting people despite differences.
- **Sports**: Sports bring a range of feelings, from excitement to frustration, offering a great way to channel energy and display your abilities. They also create a sense of belonging, linking you with others who share your interests and giving you a breather from stress and worry.
- **Dance**: Dance is a universal expression that connects cultures and languages. It's more than just moving; it's about expressing emotions like joy, sadness, and even anger. With every step, dancers share stories that resonate with people on personal, historical, and abstract levels.

*Chista, 2023. Artwork created using Midjourney.*

### Building a Soulful Foundation

Let's explore key mental skills for a better teen life. Don't worry if these are new to you; there's plenty of time to learn and grow. Lean on your family for support; take it step-by-step, and you'll be ahead in no time!

### Accountability

Do you remember when you refused to apologize after a heated argument with your parents, causing tension at home? Or when, instead of studying, you cheated on a test and got caught, resulting in disciplinary action from the school? This is why you need to develop a sense of "accountability."

Accountability is about owning your actions and realizing how they affect you and others. It's about tackling challenges, learning, and growing. Instead of blaming or dodging, it's about saying, "That was me, both the good and not-so-great."

What happens when a teen dodges responsibility?

- A teen new to accountability might rely on others for happiness or fun, missing out on developing maturity and independence.
- They might think they don't need to earn things, putting unrealistic expectations on others.

- Self-improvement and goal setting might not be their thing; they often blame past failures on external factors.
- Building and maintaining meaningful friendships can be tough when they tend to blame others.
- Feeling good about themselves and enjoying rewards just isn't the same during puberty.
- When things go wrong and parents can't step in, they find it hard to accept or understand the logical outcomes.
- In serious cases, avoiding responsibility can land a teenager in legal trouble.

Here are some tips to master this crucial skill:

- **Be in Charge**: Own up to your responsibilities. Be your own guide!
- **Clear Communication**: Stay open and honest, especially with others.
- **Ownership**: Recognize both wins and slip-ups, starting small.
- **Apologize and Learn**: Say sorry when needed, learn, and grow.
- **Avoid Blame**: Skip the blame game; think of the team and solutions.
- **Support Others**: Foster open talks, give helpful feedback, and appreciate efforts.
- **Lead by Example**: Be accountable and inspire others to do the same!

It's not about being perfect but being aware and ready to face challenges. Owning up to your actions is a big step toward soulful living.

### Resilience

Have you ever experienced feeling isolated and withdrawn after facing rejection from your friend group? Or have you found yourself dwelling on the past instead of processing your emotions and moving on positively while going through a breakup with a boyfriend? This is precisely why cultivating resilience is crucial.

Resilience is akin to your inner strength—it empowers you to bounce back stronger from adversities. It involves facing challenges head-on, learning from them, and growing as a result. But why does resilience matter?

- **Building Toughness**: Resilience toughens you up mentally and emotionally, just like training for challenges.
- **Change Expert**: You become a pro at handling new situations.
- **Learning from Setbacks:** Resilience turns setbacks into comebacks, helping you learn and grow.
- **Staying Positive**: Resilience cheers you on in tough times, reminding you of your strength.

Building resilience takes practice, so start when challenges are smaller. Here are some tips to boost your resilience and healthy coping skills:

- **Embrace Change**: Roll with it and welcome the new.
- **Keep Learning**: Focus on lessons; mistakes are stepping stones.
- **Take Tiny Risks**: Stretch your comfort zone bit by bit.
- **Practice Mindfulness:** Deep breaths or meditation calm the chaos.
- **Boost Self-Talk**: Swap negatives for "I got this; I'm tough."
- **Stay Healthy**: Sleep well, eat well, and move often.
- **Lean on Friends**: Surround yourself with good vibes and ask for help when you need it.

**INFO BIT#7:** Born in 1809 in Coupvray, France, Louis Braille lost his sight at age three in an accident. Instead of giving up, he invented the Braille system at the Royal Institute for Blind Youth in Paris—a clever way to read and write using raised dots. Despite skepticism, he perfected his system and revolutionized education for the visually impaired. Braille's story shows how setbacks can become opportunities. His resilience and determination remind us that, with passion and grit, we can make a real difference (Menon, 2023).

Building resilience is like having personal armor for life's ups and downs, preparing you for a deeper journey.

### Critical Thinking

Any memory of when you didn't critically assess your feelings before confronting your partner about a misunderstanding, resulting in a heated argument? Or when you didn't critically analyze the root causes of a disagreement with a friend, which pushed you two to unresolved tension in your relationship? "Critical thinking" would have saved you tons of stress if only you knew its tricks and hacks.

Clear thinking amid emotions is like having a mental toolbox for cloudy moments. Starting early is key! As you face bigger decisions later on, now's the perfect time to sharpen this skill with some guidance.

- Puberty gives your critical thinking a boost, helping you make smarter choices by seeing all sides.
- You'll become a creative problem-solver, tackling challenges with ease.
- As you trust your judgment more, your confidence grows, making you more self-assured in your decisions.

Here are some tips to hone this skill:

- **Spot Emotional Triggers:** Notice situations that stir strong feelings and handle them smartly.
- **Welcome Challenges**: Don't shy away from tough problems; they're chances to learn.
- **Think It Through**: Weigh up different outcomes before making decisions that match your values.

- **Be Resourceful**: Seek out reliable information; good sources are essential.
- **Seek Different Perspectives**: Connect with mentors or experts for extra insights.
- **Keep Asking Questions**: Always wonder why, how, and what if.
- **Take Time to Reflect**: Pause to consider your thoughts and actions regularly.

The aim is to get your mind in shape to make smart choices, especially when stress hits.

**Healthy Coping Mechanisms**

Feeling overwhelmed by tough situations? Coping with life's stresses is key. Practice healthy coping methods and keep a positive outlook, even when things get rough. But before we dive into tips, let's understand how stress affects your body.

Stress comes in three types: short-lived acute stress (think arguments or traffic), frequent intense events (like work deadlines), and long-lasting chronic stress (from issues like job loss or family conflicts). Regardless of the type, our bodies react with a "fight-or-flight" response, releasing hormones and speeding up our heart rate. This reaction, once useful for escaping danger, now kicks in for anything from a bear to a work deadline!

It all starts with the hypothalamus in your brain signaling the adrenal glands to release adrenaline, getting your heart racing and ready for action. If stress lingers, cortisol kicks in, affecting blood sugar and shifting your focus to stress. These hormones can cause issues if stress lasts too long, like digestive problems, weight gain, and mental health issues. Keeping stress in check is crucial to avoiding these health issues!

Here are some tips to help you manage emotions when they're running high:

- **Problem Breakdown**: Divide tasks into smaller parts for easier management and a sense of accomplishment.
- **Learn and Empower**: Gain knowledge about your challenges to feel more in control.
- **Take Deep Breaths**: Yoga, tai chi, or meditation can keep your mind Zen and zap stress and anxiety. Regular mindfulness meditation can even rewire your brain, helping you manage stress like a champ.
- **Get Moving**: Physical activity can reduce stress hormones like cortisol and increase endorphins, which are chemicals in the brain that act as natural painkillers and mood elevators. Even a simple walk or dance can release tension.
- **Healthy Eating**: Include omega-3-rich foods and veggies to manage stress hormones and maintain a balanced diet.
- **Prioritize Sleep**: Wind down before bed to ensure 7–9 hours of quality sleep, which is crucial for overall well-being.
- **Practice Gratitude**: Reflect on the good things in life daily to boost your mood and handle stress better.
- **Do What You Love**: Engage in activities that bring you joy—it's your stress-free zone.
- **Pen Your Mind**: Writing clears the cobwebs and sparks self-discovery. Expressive jotting down can ease stress and boost mood, even giving your immune system a little pep talk. So, grab that pen and let the good vibes flow!
- **Talk It Out**: Share your feelings with a trusted friend or family member for support.
- **Get Giggling!** Humor is a top-notch stress-buster. It releases feel-good endorphins, giving you a mood boost and even easing pain temporarily.
- **Cut Out Negativity**: Reduce negative influences in your media and surroundings.

- **Extend a Helping Hand**: Volunteering can be a fulfilling way to cope.
- **Social Support**: Hang out with friends or family—it's like a stress shield. Chatting with pals releases happy hormones, eases anxiety, and makes you feel all warm and fuzzy inside.
- **Nature's Healing Power**: Take a nature break! Spending time outdoors calms your mind and boosts your mood. Ever heard of forest bathing? It's like a mental spa day in the woods!
- **Music's Effect on the Brain**: Tune in and chill out! Listening to music lowers stress, calms your nerves, and puts you in a Zen state. It's like your own personal stress-relief soundtrack!
- **Art Therapy**: Get creative! Doodling, painting, or sculpting isn't just fun—it's a stress buster. Letting your artistic side loose helps you unwind and express those feelings.
- **Pet Therapy**: Furry friends to the rescue! Playing with pets boosts feel-good hormones and kicks stress to the curb. Who needs a therapist when you've got a cuddly companion?

**Listen and Observe Better!**

It might sound silly to see me listing this as a skill, but believe me, learning how to really listen and pay attention is a skill many adults can use. In the busy rush of daily life, we often forget the importance of truly hearing others. It's not just about hearing their words but also understanding their feelings and perspectives. Everyone has a story, and when we listen closely, we show we care and gain insight into the world.

Observing is like watching a silent movie of life, where every detail reveals something important. From a smile to the way someone talks, there are clues everywhere if we pay attention.

These skills help us understand people better, allowing us to connect more deeply and learn about ourselves, too. By improving our listening and observation skills, we become better at understanding others and forming meaningful relationships.

**Optimism**

Optimism, the habit of expecting good things, is a mood booster with big health perks. Research shows it slashes stress, curbs anxiety, helps heal wounds, and brings hope and comfort to those in need. Studies reveal that a sunny outlook can add years to your life, improve career success, and sweeten social connections. It's not just about a positive attitude; optimism works its magic in the brain, sparking up areas that handle mood, attention, and emotion (Shetty, 2023).

Why be optimistic? Here's the lowdown:

- **Longevity Boost**: Optimists tend to live longer, up to 15 percent longer!
- **Immune Strength:** It gives your immune system a kick, keeping those sniffles at bay.
- **Heart Happy**: Optimism lowers heart disease risk and keeps blood pressure in check.
- **Speedy Recovery**: Get back on your feet faster after surgery or illness.
- **Stress Buster**: Say goodbye to cortisol spikes with optimism on your side.
- **Social Butterfly**: Make friends easily and keep them close with your sunny disposition.
- **Problem-Solving Pro**: Tackle challenges like a boss with your optimistic mindset.
- **Academic Ace**: Score higher in school and work with persistence and positivity.
- **Mental Wellness**: Keep depression and anxiety at bay with a sunny outlook.
- **Spread the Joy**: Surround yourself with optimists and watch your mood soar!

Ready to see the world through rose-colored glasses? Embrace optimism and reap the rewards.

## Delayed Gratification

Procrastinating and cramming the night before the exam, resulting in a poor grade instead of studying consistently throughout the semester, or spending all your allowance on impulse purchases and being unable to afford something important when the need arises. Do any of the mentioned situations ring a bell?

Delayed gratification is like pressing pause on quick rewards for bigger future gains. It's about saying no to instant satisfaction for larger, long-term benefits. Self-discipline, a form of this, means keeping your eyes on the prize and choosing long-term wins over quick thrills (Strauss, 2017).

Self-discipline is crucial, and not giving it its due has caused a bunch of problems in our society:

- **Nutrition**: Fast food and unhealthy snacks have led to serious health problems for about 38 percent of Americans.
- **Physical Pleasures**: From 2016 to 2020, drug use among 8th graders jumped by 61 percent. Plus, 62 percent of high school seniors have sipped alcohol, and half have dabbled in drugs.

Ever heard of Walter Mischel's "marshmallow studies?" Picture preschoolers resisting marshmallows for bigger rewards later. It turns out that those with strong willpower not only rocked academically but also aced stress tests compared to the marshmallow-grabbers.

Mastering delayed gratification helps teens in several ways:

- **Social Life**: Balancing fun and long-term goals, like academics, instead of partying nonstop.
- **Success**: Staying focused, avoiding distractions, and aiming for lasting achievements.
- **Money Matters**: Saving for the future instead of spending on impulse buys.

Instant gratification is tempting, but holding out for long-term rewards is a valuable skill. Here are some tips to help you resist those quick wins:

- **Set Clear Goals**: Knowing what you want down the road helps you resist quick fixes.
- **Distract Yourself**: Shift your focus to other enjoyable things.
- **Wait 24 Hours**: Simple but effective. Try adding items to your cart and waiting a day before buying. You might find that your cart remains abandoned.
- **Envision Your Future Self**: Daydream about your future self and your long-term goals.
- **Practice Gratitude**: Being thankful makes waiting easier.
- **Find a Role Model**: Look up to someone who can boost your patience for bigger goals.
- **Reward Yourself**: Treat yourself when you reach milestones; it makes waiting worth it!

Challenging yourself with longer goals fits the idea that practice makes perfect. Getting comfortable with discomfort during your teen years sets you up for a future where smart choices and big wins go hand in hand.

**INFO BIT#8:** IQ or EQ? Is success more about book smarts or street smarts? That's the IQ vs. EQ debate in a nutshell. IQ focuses on cognitive abilities like reasoning and memory, while EQ hones in on emotional skills like recognizing and managing feelings, both yours and others. Nowadays, EQ is in the spotlight, especially in business and education. Companies value it for hiring and leadership, and schools are incorporating EQ programs into their curricula. Both IQ and EQ aren't set in stone. They can be influenced by factors like upbringing, education, and health. But the good news is that you can boost both. For IQ, think memory exercises and learning new languages. For EQ, try practicing self-awareness, empathy, and mindfulness. Ultimately, while IQ was once considered the main predictor of success, it's becoming clear that EQ is just as vital for navigating life, relationships, and careers. In the last chapter, we'll explore how the brain can change its synaptic paths to accommodate new habits and data.

## CHAPTER ACTIVITIES

### Accountability Buddy System

Team up with a buddy for accountability.
Set goals and check in often to track progress and support each other. It's a great way to boost responsibility and encourage each other's growth!

### Resilience Diary

Start a resilience diary to record moments of strength during tough times, using writing, drawings, or collages. Share entries with friends and discuss how resilience shapes your growth.

### Critical Thinking Escape Room

Try an escape room activity with friends, or visit one nearby. Work in teams to solve puzzles that test critical thinking and teamwork, helping you hone problem-solving skills and understand different perspectives.

### Delayed Gratification Challenge

Try a delayed gratification experiment: Set a short-term goal, resist immediate rewards, and think about the process. It's a great way to learn patience and see the benefits of working toward your goals!

*Coping Mechanisms Exploration*

Try out healthy coping methods like deep breathing, exercise, or gratitude practices. Keep a journal to track your experiences and share insights with others, discussing what works best for you and exploring new ideas from fellow readers.

## LIGHTBULB MOMENT

In the journey of finding yourself, embracing what makes you special is key to thriving. Focus on well-being over looks and build a strong and authentic base. Learning important skills like taking responsibility, bouncing back from setbacks, and dealing with stress leads to a brighter path filled with hope and the joys of waiting for good things.

Next up, we'll share simple tips for positive social vibes—hanging out with friends, handling colleagues, or spending time with your significant other.

# NAVIGATING THE SOCIAL MAZE

 *Things are never quite as scary when you've got a best friend.*

— BILL WATTERSON

Talking socials: I feel like expectations from us are always changing based on different situations and times. Chasing social trends and standards feels like a hamster on a wheel. Staying relevant while growing up can be a challenge on top of everything else we are going through!

I've always been shy since childhood, wishing I could blend into the background behind me. Immigration only intensified my fears since I was also unsure about the culture. Suddenly, I had the freedom to express myself, dress however I liked in public, and make new connections—be me. While exciting, this new life also brought a sense of uncertainty about almost everything I did. In particular, I was very anxious not to mess things up with my non-Persian friends: "How do I make friends with people from different backgrounds than mine?"

Eventually, I was invited to dinner at a work friend's house, which led to me bombarding her with questions on how to handle the night. She just stared at me with a blank face. "Just be yourself," she said with a smile. What horrible advice! If only she knew that being me meant hearing my laughs from three blocks away! Besides the fact that I wasn't sure how to be myself without stepping on anyone's toes, the idea of offending her family absolutely terrified me.

Doing research about social etiquette got me into an arena called "Communication Studies." Digging deep into it made me feel better since I realized my fears weren't uncommon; many people struggle with social anxiety. I discovered useful tools and "rules" that can benefit anyone looking to socialize better. So, this chapter kicks off with insights I want to share—not because I assume you're socially awkward, but to help you navigate the ever-changing social scene more confidently. Let's begin by discussing how to break the ice.

## BREAKING THE ICE

Ever felt the pressure of making a killer first impression but not sure how to start a chat? Mastering the art of breaking the ice is the trick! Once you ace that initial meet-up, keeping the convo flowing is a breeze. Let's dive into the secrets of making a stellar first impression!

## DRESS CODE

When dressing for social events, consider the dress code. Do you want to win over your besties' parents? Opt for something more modest. It's all about finding the right balance between your personal style and what fits the occasion. So, if your go-to is "as cozy as possible," but you're off to a wedding, ditch the sweats. Aim for a stylish yet comfy semi-formal look. Remember, dressing appropriately doesn't mean sacrificing comfort. Respect the event's vibe while staying true to yourself.

The power of a killer outfit in job interviews, networking events, and first dates—your attire speaks volumes about your professionalism and confidence. Here are some essential tips to make sure you're making a positive impression:

- **Dress Sharp**: Well-fitted clothes instantly elevate your look. If they're not quite right, consider tailoring for that extra polish.
- **Stay Neat and Tidy**: Wrinkles and dirt? No thanks! Take a few minutes to iron and ensure your clothes are clean. Oh, and don't skimp on appropriate underwear!
- **Splash of Color**: Choose hues that match your mood—dark shades for a pro vibe, lighter tones for a laid-back, creative feel.
- **Accessorize Smart**: Jazz up your outfit with a watch, scarf, or bag, but keep it subtle. Remember, less is more!
- **Comfort Is Key**: Wear clothes that make you feel great. Confidence comes from comfort, and it reflects in your demeanor.

## POLITENESS

When you start chatting, don't skip the niceties. Being polite is key to making a good first impression and bonding with others. It's about showing respect, empathy, and kindness—qualities everyone appreciates in personal and professional talks. To keep it polite, here's the deal:

- **Respect**: Treat others well; it goes far.
- **Empathy**: Put yourself in their shoes—it makes a difference.
- **Gratitude**: Saying thanks, even for small stuff, is nice.
- **Handling Conflict**: Approach disagreements with kindness, respect, and empathy.
- **Apologize and Forgive**: Embrace apologies and forgiveness— it's all part of being human.

Now, let's dive into how politeness adds flavor to those first meetings:

- **Warm Greetings**: A genuine smile, a friendly handshake, and eye contact show warmth and interest.
- **Language**: Choose words wisely. Polite language shows respect. Save the jargon, slang, and super casual talk for more laid-back settings.
- **Stay Positive**: Even in tricky situations, staying cool, polite, and respectful shows off your professionalism and composure.

## ETIQUETTE

Want to nail that first impression? Etiquette's your ticket. It's like a guidebook for how we interact. Get it down pat, and you'll come off polished, professional, and plain nice. Etiquette covers a bunch, like:

- **Greetings and Introductions**: Say hi and introduce yourself —the basics of making a good entrance.
- **Conversation and Communication**: Know when to chat, when to listen, and how to speak without going overboard.
- **Dining Etiquette**: Don't panic at the table. Learn the dos and don'ts of dining like a champ.

Sure, some of this comes with time, but here are a few must-dos to kick you off:

- **Show Some Gratitude**: A simple "thanks" goes a long way. Acknowledge acts of kindness and help.
- **Give a Hand**: Help out when needed. It's a small gesture with a big impact.
- **Own Up to Mistakes**: We all goof up. Take responsibility, apologize when necessary, and move on.
- **Consider Others**: Be aware of others' needs and feelings in your interactions. It's just good manners.

## CULTURAL SENSITIVITY

Ever heard of cultural sensitivity? It's the art of understanding and respecting different cultures and beliefs, which is crucial for making a great first impression. Here's how to ace the cultural sensitivity game:

- **Check Your Biases**: We all have cultural biases—those ideas and beliefs we get from our own culture. Knowing them helps you avoid making assumptions about others.
- **Show Respect to All Cultures**: Take a little time to learn about other cultures and their customs. It's like having a cheat sheet to understand why people do what they do.
- **Keep an Open Mind**: Embrace new experiences. Be willing to try things you've never tried before, and be open to having your own views challenged.
- **Ditch the Generalizations**: Not everyone from a culture is the same. Avoid painting everyone with the same brush, and steer clear of assuming based on a few encounters.

## BODY LANGUAGE

Body language is key to making a great first impression. It can shout confidence, openness, and trustworthiness or scream nervousness, disinterest, or even dishonesty. So, let's get the body language game on point:

- **Lock Eyes**: Keep your eye contact natural; aim for 60 to 70 percent.
- **Smile Like You Mean It**: A genuine smile is a game-changer. Your face is like a billboard—make sure it's advertising warmth and approachability.
- **Posture**: Stand tall, relax your shoulders, and hold your head high. It screams confidence, unlike slouching, which sends vibes of insecurity.

- **Hand Gestures**: Open-palm gestures show warmth. Keep it open, ditch the fidgety moves, and show you're at ease.
- **Mirroring**: Subtly copy body language for connection, but don't overdo it.
- **Mind the Gap**: Find that sweet spot when it comes to personal space. Respect boundaries, find a comfortable distance, and remember that invading or standing too far away is a no-go.
- **Active Listening**: Nod, lean in, and maintain eye contact to show you're engaged.

Remember, body language speaks volumes without saying a word. With practice and awareness, you can master it. Pay attention, adjust, and see how your body language enhances your first impressions.

TABLE MANNERS

*Chista, 2023. Artwork created using Midjourney.*

Table manners are like your dining playbook, especially when you've got company. From handling utensils to keeping the chatter lively, these manners aren't just details—they make a big impression. Here's the lowdown on mealtime manners:

- **Utensil Wisdom**: Hold those utensils right, cut your food into bite-sized pieces, and keep the clatter to a minimum. No one wants a dining companion creating a symphony with their fork.

- **Chew and Swallow with Class**: Mouth closed, no slurping, and definitely no noisy food performances. Chew, swallow, then take another bite—it's the rhythm of mealtime.
- **Posture Perfection**: Sit up straight, avoid leaning on the table, and keep the conversation pleasant. Good posture shows you're fully engaged, not just lounging around.
- **Napkin Basics**: Use your napkin to wipe your mouth and hands, place it neatly on your lap, and dig into your meal. Napkins aren't just for show; they're your cleanup crew.
- **Pass the Dishes Smoothly**: Pass dishes like a pro—from left to right, with no stretching across the table, and offer to serve before diving into your own plate. It's like a well-coordinated dance routine.
- **Polite Departures**: If you need a break, ask to step away and return promptly once you're finished. Nobody likes an empty seat for too long.
- **Say Thank You**: Show genuine gratitude to your host. Appreciate the meal and the hospitality—it's the cherry on top of good manners.

Follow these dining rules, and you're not just breaking the ice; you're laying the groundwork for a perfect first impression. But hey, not all relationships are forever, especially in a toxic dining situation.

**INFO BIT#9:** Scan the below QR code to learn more about the table setting 101 rules.

## SETTING BOUNDARIES

Let's talk boundaries—a key part of adulting. They're like sturdy walls, protecting your well-being from chaos by preventing you from feeling overwhelmed or taken advantage of. Here are some tips for creating solid boundaries to safeguard your inner peace:

- **Know Your Needs**: Reflect on your values versus what drains your energy, makes you uneasy, or messes with your boundaries.
- **Timing Is Everything**: No drama-filled chats in public. Keep it chill and private.
- **"I" Statements Rule**: Express your needs using "I" statements. Skip the blame game. Instead of "You always talk over me," try "I feel unheard when you interrupt me."
- **Crystal Clear Instructions**: No room for vagueness. Clearly lay out your boundaries. Instead of "I need more space," say, "Let's not hang out every weekend. I need some solo time to recharge."
- **Firm Yet Friendly**: Be nice, but don't budge on what you need.
- **Anticipate Pushback:** Your friend might not instantly jump on the boundary bandwagon. Give them time to process. Be patient, but stay firm.
- **Keep Enforcing**: Stick to your guns. Say no when needed, remind your friend, and limit interactions if necessary. Consistency is key.
- **Get Backup**: If the boundary game gets tough, reach for therapists or counselors to guide you, boost your communication skills, and have your back.

Remember, boundaries are a journey, not a one-time fix. Adjust as needed, and don't forget: You're worth the respect, girl!

## NAVIGATING PEER PRESSURE

Struggling to fit in because everyone else is doing it? Trust me, it's a common teen dilemma. All that pressure to fit in and be "attractive" by society's rules can mess with your uniqueness, self-acceptance, and real happiness. Here's why it's cool to resist and rock your own style:

- **Unrealistic Standards**: Those social media beauty standards? Total fantasy. Trying to keep up can mess with your head and distort what real beauty is.
- **Blocks Self-Discovery**: Real happiness comes from being yourself, not what others expect. Focusing too much on what others think can totally block your journey to self-discovery.
- **Unhealthy Habits**: Trying to fit a certain look might lead to not-so-great habits like extreme dieting or cosmetic procedures, which can mess with both your body and mind.
- **Embracing Your Quirks Boosts Self-Love**: Confidence starts flowing when you embrace your unique look. It makes you shine from the inside out.
- **True Beauty Is You Being You**—not fitting some mold. It's about rocking your individuality and giving off confidence that's your unique self.

Ready to crush peer pressure with style? Here's how:

- **Stick to Your Values**: Trust your gut and make choices based on what you believe in. Be your own boss against social pressure.
- **Question Beauty Standards**: Those flawless pics? Not reality. Stay critical and keep it real.
- **Surround Yourself with Positivity**: Hang out with people who love you for being you. Positive vibes help you stay strong against peer pressure.
- **Be Kind to Yourself**: Embrace your imperfections. Being kind to yourself reduces stress and boosts confidence.
- **Celebrate Diversity and Promote Body Positivity**: Spread the word—bodies come in all shapes and sizes, and that's awesome. Let's celebrate being different!

Your true beauty shines when you embrace your quirks, ooze confidence, and keep it real. Resisting peer pressure opens doors to a life filled with fulfillment and self-love. Rocking your own style is just the beginning. Go on, be your own cheerleader—you've got this!

## TOXIC VS. HEALTHY RELATIONSHIPS

Healthy friendships are all about good vibes, respect, and growing together. Here's what to look for:

- **Mutual Respect**: Partners appreciate each other's feelings, opinions, and quirks. It's all about kindness and consideration.
- **Open Communication**: No secrets! Partners chat openly, honestly, and without fear of judgment.
- **Trust and Support**: They've got each other's backs through thick and thin.
- **Healthy Conflict Resolution**: Disagreements don't turn into a battleground. Partners work through issues constructively.
- **Personal Growth and Shared Goals**: They support each other's dreams while pursuing common goals.

Now, onto the dark side of the spectrum:

- **Unhealthy Communication**: Think of yelling and emotional shutdowns. Effective conflict resolution? Not on the menu.
- **Lack of Respect**: One partner tunes out the other's needs, creating a disrespectful vibe.
- **Control and Manipulation**: One partner pulls the strings, using manipulation or guilt trips.
- **Constant Criticism**: One partner is the constant rain cloud. Complaints, gossip, belittling—it's a negativity overload.
- **Dishonesty and Betrayal**: Trust goes out the window with lies or cheating.
- **Jealousy and Competition**: A toxic friend might feel threatened by your success and try to bring you down.

- **Gaslighting**: Messing with your head and making you doubt reality.
- **Lack of Empathy**: Your feelings? Who cares? A toxic friend may lack understanding, leaving you feeling isolated.
- **One-Sided Effort**: You're doing all the heavy lifting.
- **Emotional Rollercoaster**: Happy one moment, hurt or angry the next. A toxic friendship is a wild ride.
- **Energy Drain**: Hanging out leaves you wiped out.

Toxic friendships take a toll. Spotting signs isn't always easy, but tuning into your feelings and how things are going can help. If you notice these red flags, talk to someone you trust. A therapist or counselor can help you see patterns and figure out how to handle them. Just remember, you deserve friendships that lift you up and treat you right!

## CRACKING THE DATING CODE: DOS AND DON'TS

When it comes to dating, it's like navigating a funky dance floor—there are moves to bust and others to avoid. Let's break it down and explore the basics.

### *The Dos*

- **Be Yourself**: No need for theatrics. Just be you; the right person will dig it.
- **Be Respectful**: Treat your date with kindness, even if the chemistry isn't sparking. Keep your standards up, and, if needed, gracefully excuse yourself.
- **Listen Up**: Tone down the nervous jabber and tune in to your date's story. Let them take the mic and see where the conversation flows.
- **Ask Away**: Show you're interested by asking about their life, hobbies, and values. It's all about the getting-to-know-you game.

- **Stay Positive**: Keep the vibe light and breezy. Ditch the complaints and focus on making the date enjoyable.
- **Phone Down**: Stick that phone in your pocket; your date deserves your full focus. Instagram can wait; this moment can't.
- **Offer to Pay**: If you're the one who set up the date, offering to cover the tab is a classy move. If they want to split, go with the flow or discuss it together.
- **Thank Your Date**: Express gratitude for their time and let them know if you had a good time.

*The Don'ts*

- **No Ex-Talk**: Keep the ex-files closed. Your date doesn't need a history lesson.
- **Don't Overshare**: Hold back on the personal info dump. Oversharing can be overwhelming.
- **Be Cool to the Staff**: How you treat the waitstaff says a lot about you. Keep it classy.
- **Respect Boundaries**: Respect their boundaries. Physical intimacy should be a mutual decision, not a pressured one.
- **Be On Time**: Punctuality shows respect. Don't leave them hanging.
- **Don't Be a Know-It-All**: Leave room for surprises. Nobody wants a walking encyclopedia. Embrace the chance to learn from your date.
- **Have Fun**: Loosen up! Dating should be a good time, not a stress-fest.

Now, let's tackle something crucial: consent and boundaries. It's a bit awkward, but trust me, it's worth chatting about.

*Dating Wisdom: Consent and Boundaries*

*Chista, 2023. Artwork created using Midjourney.*

In the dating game, you've got two MVPs on your team: consent and boundaries. They're like your personal bodyguards, guiding you through the scene and keeping your feelings and space safe. Talking about them might feel awkward, but it's crucial for a smooth dating ride.

- **Consent Unpacked**: Consent means a solid "yes" to anything intimate. Your partner needs your enthusiastic agreement before moving forward, no matter what. Your feelings matter, and saying "no" is totally okay. Have an honest chat with your partner about your limits upfront. Remember, silence doesn't equal consent, and it's okay to change your mind.
- **Getting Boundary Savvy**: Boundaries come in all shapes and sizes. Personal space is key—respect each other's bubble and ask before getting touchy. Emotional boundaries matter, too; no pressure or games are allowed. Discuss your limits with your partner to keep respect and trust strong. Need a hand starting the conversation? Talk to a cool older friend or a trusted adult. You don't have to figure it out alone!

**INFO BIT#10:** Let's dive into the online dating pool—a rollercoaster ride in the American dating scene. According to the Pew Research Center, a whopping 30 percent of Americans hopped on board in 2023. Now, here's the lowdown: Most dating apps skip background checks, so it's up to you to spot the shady characters. Experts say even with background checks, total safety is a stretch since, sadly, sexual assaults often go unreported. Like any blind date, digital or in-person, it's smart to have some tricks up your sleeve for safer swiping. Now, onto the nitty-gritty of online connections:

- Avoid those overfiltered, duck-faced selfies you flaunt on social media. Believe me, you don't want your date uncovering your Insta in two clicks flat. Ditch the live photos—they practically come with a built-in GPS tracker, making it too easy for someone to tail your every move.
- Keep your personal deets to yourself. Don't share your sensitive info, and if they start fishing for cash, reel yourself back in—ASAP!
- Stalking is wrong, but a quick social media check before a date is totally fair game. You might wonder about the double standards; I hear you. Well, I'm here to protect you! And trust me, running a predate detective mission to ensure your potential date isn't actually a catfish lurking behind a fake profile, fair or not, has become a bit of a dating ritual. So, until the rules change, it seems like a quick social media check is here to stay!
- When it's time to meet up, video chat is your best bet. And for the real deal, stick to public spots—no cozy Netflix and chill sessions at your place! Make sure your date is legit before diving into that cringy coffee outing. Always let a friend know where you're headed and toss 'em your date's pic—just in case. Trust your gut; if something feels off, it probably is. Don't leave your drink unattended, either. Stick to what feels right, even if it means sipping your drink slower. If your date doesn't get that safety's top priority, they can hit the road. You don't need someone clueless about basic courtesy, right? And if things get sticky, call in the bartender or waiter! They're your trusty sidekick, whether it's creating a diversion, calling

for backup, or getting you a safe ride home. Think of them as your personal bodyguard in a pinch!

- Stay independent—don't count on your date for wheels. Keep those ride-share apps handy in case you need a quick getaway plan. Remember, knowing your boundaries is cool. Keep your smarts sharp, and don't let anyone push you into stuff you're not feeling.
- Listen to your instincts. If a profile looks fishy, it's probably a faker. Use your detective skills wisely. Don't buy into financial sob stories, vague responses, or vanishing acts—you're too savvy for that. If you run into any sketchy characters, don't hesitate to block and report them to help out others.

And if all else fails, you've always got the power to unmatch, block, and report. Remember, your manners can wait; your safety can't!

## CHAPTER ACTIVITIES

### Icebreaker Extravaganza

Organize a fun icebreaker event to help everyone connect. Whether it's sharing fun facts or playing games, the aim is to make socializing easy and enjoyable!

### Cultural Sensitivity Showcase

Host a cultural sensitivity fair featuring food tasting, art displays, and discussions to explore different cultures, traditions, and customs and break cultural stereotypes.

*Dining Decorum Discovery*

Try a mock dinner with friends or family to practice table manners, from using utensils to polite chat. Think about how these manners help you make a good impression in social situations.

*Defining Your Relationship Compass*

Craft a list of your relationship boundaries, whether you're dating or not. It's important to know your physical and emotional limits beforehand. Keep this list handy and check it often. Remember to communicate your boundaries when needed.

*Empathy Builders Workshop*

Let's shape change together!

 a. Talk about empathy and its power to spark positive change.
 b. Share personal stories and ideas about empathy.
 c. Research societal issues in teams and share what you find.
 d. Think of volunteer opportunities that match your interests.
 e. Make plans to make a difference in your community!

*Independence vs. Togetherness Activity*

Create a worksheet with two columns: "Independence" and "Togetherness." List activities you enjoy alone and those you prefer with others. Discuss how balancing independence and togetherness is key to a healthy relationship.

LIGHTBULB MOMENT

We've covered social dynamics, from starting conversations to healthy relationships and dating tips. With a better understanding of consent and boundaries, you're ready for smoother social interactions.

Next up: tackling bullying. Whether you've dealt with it or not, the next chapter's insights could help support others in tough times. Let's empower you to make a difference in your life and others. Ready to dive in?

# FROM HURT TO HEALING

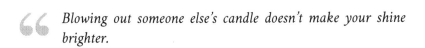
*Blowing out someone else's candle doesn't make your shine brighter.*

— UNKNOWN

I completed a grueling 1,500-hour internship to qualify for the pharmacy board test. Switching from the old-school pharmacy system in Iran to electronic systems in the U.S. felt like trying to juggle flaming torches. To top it off, processing prescriptions at a long-term care pharmacy, where medications were processed and packed on set schedules, made it even harder since I had zero training in processing. Meanwhile, there was this coworker who blamed every problem on me, even on my days off!

Discovering a good HR setup at my new job was like finding a golden ticket. I realized that my old gig was more blind than a bat to bullying, likely just to avoid drama. I am sharing my tale now to lend a hand to anyone in a similar pickle. Just a reminder: Respect is nonnegotiable —no ifs, ands, or buts. At the end of the day, we're all just equal human beings.

In this chapter, let's tackle the big B-word: bullying. We've all accidentally stepped on some toes, so it's important to be nice and avoid turning into bullies ourselves. And if you've been on the receiving end, it's all about healing. Remember, kindness beats bullying every time!

*Chista, 2023. Artwork created using Midjourney.*

## UNDERSTANDING BULLYING

Bullying involves aggressive behavior aimed at hurting or controlling someone through physical, verbal, social, or cyber means. It's often subtler than depicted in the media, with four main types as outlined by the Australian Human Rights Commission:

- **Physical Bullying**: When someone uses hitting or shoving to be a jerk.
- **Verbal Bullying**: When name-calling and teasing are the weapons of choice.
- **Social Bullying**: When gossip and rumors are used to leave someone out.
- **Cyberbullying**: When nasty messages or comments are posted online.

Between 15 and 22 percent of students have to deal with this nonsense, according to the bigwigs at the Department of Education and the CDC. It's such a big deal that they're practically begging for more programs to stop it from happening. Let's face it: no one wants to deal with a bully, whether it's on the playground or in the class-room. Understanding bullies helps us deal with them better. They're not always just bad eggs; there's often more to the story. This doesn't excuse their behavior, but it helps us see their side. Here's why kids and teens might bully:

- **To Feel Powerful**: Some bully to feel bigger and stronger when they lack control in their own lives.
- **To Fit In**: Bullying can be a way to belong and be accepted by a group.
- **For Attention**: Some crave any attention, even a negative kind.
- **For Fun**: Sadly, some find pleasure in hurting others.
- **To Vent Frustration**: It can be an outlet for anger or frustration.
- **Copying Others**: Some learn bullying from adults around them, like parents or teachers.

If you've faced bullying, it's not your fault. Their actions say more about them than you. Appreciate your uniqueness and remember that you're cared for. Now, let's talk about handling bullies.

## DEALING WITH BULLIES

Dealing with bullies is tough and stressful, but standing up for your-self is important. Here are some strategies to handle bullying and protect yourself:

- **Stay Calm**: Bullies love reactions. Keeping your cool takes away their power.
- **Communicate Clearly:** Be assertive but respectful. Firmly tell them, "Stop treating me like that."

- **Avoid Engagement**: Don't argue or defend yourself; it can make things worse. Try walking away, ignoring them, or changing the subject instead.
- **Document Incidents**: Keep a record of bullying incidents with dates, times, and details. It's useful for reporting.
- **Practice Self-Care**: Focus on activities like exercise, meditation, or spending time outside to manage stress.
- **Seek Support**: Talk to trusted adults like teachers or parents. Surround yourself with supportive friends and family.
- **Consider Professional Help**: If bullying is severe or distressing, reach out to a therapist or counselor.

You're not alone in dealing with bullying. Support is available to help you manage it, stay safe, and come out stronger.

## HELP, I'VE BEEN THE BULLY

Hey, if you've realized you might have been the bully, no judgment here. We're not about making you feel bad; chances are, you already do. Let's focus on what to do next. Admitting this shows your accountability, which is a big step toward a positive change. Here's a guide for teens in this situation:

- **Admit what you did**. Own up to your actions and acknowledge they were hurtful.
- **Take responsibility**. No dodging or excuses—just own it and genuinely feel sorry.
- **Say sorry, for real**. Reach out to those you hurt and apologize sincerely.
- **Reflect on why**. Figure out why you went down the bullying path—was it for power or fitting in?
- **Learn from your mistakes**. Grow from this experience and commit to being more respectful and considerate.
- **Practice empathy**. Put yourself in their shoes to avoid causing harm and build stronger connections.

- **Don't go it alone**. If you're struggling, talk to trusted adults for guidance and support.
- **Be an anti-bully advocate**. Use what you've learned to stand up against hurtful behavior and make a positive impact.

Remember, change starts with self-awareness and the commitment to do better. Embrace growth, learn from mistakes, and let your actions speak louder than your past.

## CYBERBULLYING AND ONLINE SAFETY

*Chista, 2023. Artwork created using Midjourney.*

Cyberbullying is basically online bullying, like sending mean messages or embarrassing posts. Here's what to watch out for:

- Sending hurtful texts or emails.
- Posting embarrassing content on social media.
- Spreading rumors or lies online.
- Making fake profiles to harass.
- Excluding folks from online groups or activities.

Cyberbullying can be a real downer, messing with your vibe and bringing on all sorts of stress. But fear not! Here are some simple ways to keep your online world safe and sound:

- **Guard Your Info**: Keep those passwords strong, use multifactor authentication, encryption, and strong passwords, and don't spill all the beans on social media.

- **Privacy Is Key**: Tweak those social media settings to control who sees your posts. Stick to accepting friend requests from folks you know and trust. Quality over quantity, right?
- **Armor Up**: Get yourself some solid antivirus software to keep those cyber nasties at bay. Keep your system and software updated with the latest security patches. Think of it like giving your devices a cyber shield.
- **Think before You Post**: Once it's out there, it's out there. So, think twice before hitting that share button.
- **Stranger Danger**: No diving into private conversations or meeting up with online pals without some serious precautions.
- **Click Wisely**: Sketchy links? No thanks! Avoid clicking on anything that seems fishy. You don't want to end up swimming in malware.
- **Fight Back**: If you spot it, report it. Use tools to filter out nasty stuff, and don't join in on the negativity.
- **Spread the Love**: Be a beacon of kindness online. It's contagious, you know? Let's make the digital world a happier place, one nice comment at a time.

Remember, your online safety is in your hands. By using these practical tips, you're not just looking out for yourself but also making the digital world safer and happier for everyone. Stay alert, be kind, and enjoy the online space responsibly.

**INFO BIT#11:** An ACE is like that cringe-worthy moment in seventh grade when you got mocked over your parents' divorce rumors. Getting bullied or feeling neglected sticks with you like gum on your shoe. It can mess with the victim's sense of safety. Scientists have found out that bullying can affect areas that handle emotions like the amygdala and prefrontal cortex, messing with how your brain talks to itself and making it harder to understand feelings and keep them in check. This ramps up stress hormones like cortisol and weakens your immune system, leading to inflammation, depression, and even medical conditions like hypertension and obesity. According to a 2013 study in JAMA Psychiatry, both bullies and their victims are more likely to have childhood psychiatric disorders like anxiety and depression. Surprisingly, it's the bullies—not their targets—who are at a higher risk of developing antisocial personality disorder later in life. But here's the twist: most bullies have been bullied themselves, creating a vicious cycle. It's like a mean-spirited game of tag that nobody wants to play.

Now, hear the good news: no one's brain is set in stone! The brain's capability called "neuroplasticity"—which will be discussed in the last chapter—helps it bounce back, adapt, and change over time. So, even if you've dealt with bullying, it doesn't mean you're doomed to a lifetime of health issues.

## DIGITAL FOOTPRINT

Your digital footprint is like leaving behind breadcrumbs online. Every post, comment, or site visit shapes your online reputation, affecting how others see you, especially potential employers. A positive footprint highlights your skills, while a negative one can send the wrong message. Here's why it counts:

- **Job Seekers**: Employers often snoop around online profiles. A positive digital footprint can show off your professionalism and interests.
- **College Admissions**: Admissions officers may take a peek at your online presence. A well-kept digital footprint can give your application a boost.
- **Future Relationships**: People might check out your profiles before connecting. A positive digital footprint can help attract friends or partners.

Just remember, your digital footprint is like your online mirror. By being careful about what you post and taking steps to manage it, you can leave a positive and lasting impression.

## CHAPTER ACTIVITIES

### Reflective Journaling

Let's have some journaling fun again! Get your journal and write about bullying, self-discovery, and personal growth. It's your space to reflect and grow—let the scribbling start!

### Bystander to Upstander Contest

We're transforming bystanders into upstanders against bullying. Check out different bullying scenarios, brainstorm ways to help the victim, act out your ideas, talk about any obstacles, and listen to uplifting stories of standing up to bullying.

Here's my story: Once, I spotted two guys taunting a hedgehog on campus. I couldn't just watch; I spoke up and made them stop. With the campus guard's assistance, we safely moved the hedgehog back to nature. Remember, bullying is never okay, regardless of the victim.

### Collaborative Anti-Bullying Mural

Let's dive into the art world and join forces to paint a mural, imagining a world without bullying. Each person can add their special touch to the canvas, creating a masterpiece that celebrates kindness and unity. It'll be a creative experience to remember!

### Digital Footprint Audit

Let's casually scroll through our socials! Notice any oversharing or cringy digital footprints? Let's brainstorm quick fixes to tidy up.

Share tips, have a laugh, and, together, we'll make our digital space feel cozy and secure. Ready for a relaxed digital makeover?

### Random Acts of Digital Kindness Challenge

Get ready to spread digital sunshine! Challenge each other with positive comments and heartwarming shares. After this kindness burst, share your reflections—it's a virtual group hug!

## LIGHTBULB MOMENT

We addressed bullying by focusing on kindness and awareness. We discussed ways to deal with bullies and stay safe online—remember, strong passwords count!

Now, let's dive into balancing school, fun, and self-care. Beat procrastination, crush distractions, and make the most of your time!

# TIME MANAGEMENT

 *Time is really the only capital that any human being has, and the only thing he can't afford to lose.*

— THOMAS EDISON

Let's kick things off with a classic Edison quote that's stuck with me forever. Back in my teens, I thought I had time management down pat, but boy, was I wrong! If only I could hop into a time machine and give my younger self a crash course on what really matters. Since time travel is not an option, I'm passing on this wisdom to my six-year-old son, hoping he'll catch on early. Ready to dive into the time management rabbit hole with me?

Let's keep it simple. Time management, according to the Cambridge Dictionary, is all about using your time wisely, especially at work. But here's my two cents: Without nailing it, chasing your dreams can feel like a game of cat and mouse, setting you up for a flop. Here's why:

Back in school, poor time management meant falling behind on homework, skipping extracurriculars, and saying goodbye to your social life. But hold your horses. As life piles on responsibilities, poor time management can stir up trouble, even messing with your future job prospects. Here's why.

- **Decreased Productivity**: No boss ever said, "I love consistent poor performance." It's a surefire way to miss out on promotions and career growth despite your efforts.
- **Strained Work Relationships**: Would you like a colleague who only brings delays or disruptions to the table? You certainly wouldn't, so they won't either.
- **Financial Consequences**: Late payments and inefficient budgeting would cause you to find yourself financially poor despite probably working hard.
- **Increased Stress at Work**: Well, let's put it this way: stress would never ever leave you alone.
- **Work-Life Balance?** Forget it.

Hold up; we've got more ground to cover. Let's tackle the pitfalls of poor management in your role as a parent:

- **Stress and Burnout**: Juggling the myriad responsibilities of parenthood would feel like running a marathon with no finish line in sight.
- **Missed Milestones**: Blink, and you might miss important moments in your child's life, from school events to recitals, each a precious memory in the making.
- **Negative Role Model**: Perhaps the most dreaded consequence is that passing on poor time management habits to the next generation feels like dropping the ball on a legacy.
- **Poor Family Relationships**: Quality time and effective communication with family members suffer, which can strain the very bonds that are meant to support you.

Let's talk some eye-opening statistics if you're still not convinced:

- Eighty-eight percent of working folks procrastinate on the regular.
- Around 31.9 percent fess up to procrastinating for two to three hours daily.
- A hefty 17 percent admit they waste up to four hours daily due to repeatedly putting off tasks.
- The average worker spends 51 percent of every workday on low to no-value tasks.

Life's like a game of chess, full of moves and grooves. Why wait around? Learning this skill early sets the stage for ace grades, top-notch jobs, and stellar parenting. Getting a head start isn't just about acing school; it's about shaping our destiny. But there's no need to stress—it's never too late. Grab the bull by the horns for the life you crave. And when I say now, I mean NOW!

*Chista, 2023. Artwork created using Midjourney.*

## WHAT'S YOUR STYLE?

Before we get into the time management stuff, let's figure out your style (Martin, 2020). It's like finding the perfect dance move for you. Let's check out these time management vibes and their nifty tips. Sounds good?

- **Hopper**: Multitasking maestro? Let's boost that productivity.

- Pros: You're a multitasking marvel!
- Cons: Multitasking might not be as smart as we think, possibly making you less sharp and muddling your organization.
- Tips for Success: Ditch distractions, try the Pomodoro technique, and prioritize tasks.

- **Cliffhanger**: Love the adrenaline rush? Time to take it easy.

  - Pros: You handle stress like a boss.
  - Cons: Rushed work and procrastination tendencies.
  - Tips for Success: Track your time, prioritize tasks, and set earlier deadlines. Stress-free work? Sign us up!

- **Big Picture**: More forest, fewer trees? Quick thinker, but don't skip the details.

  - Pros: Creative problem-solving is your jam.
  - Cons: Missing the small stuff, risking quality.
  - Tips for Success: Stick to a routine, team up with detail-oriented pals, and speak clearly.

- **Perfectionist**: Quality over quantity, but don't forget that time's ticking.

  - Pros: Top-notch work, always.
  - Cons: Risking deadlines.
  - Tips for Success: Mix up tasks, set realistic plans, and handle time wisely. Delegate when needed and avoid sweating the small stuff.

- **Impulsive**: Spontaneous? Structure wouldn't hurt.

  - Pros: Thriving in unexpected situations.
  - Cons: Long-term focus might be a struggle.
  - Tips for Success: Add some routine, make plans, and schedule spontaneity.

- **The Early Bird**: You're the checklist champ, diving in headfirst.

  - Pros: Smashing goals and staying motivated.
  - Cons: Speedy work might miss the details.
  - Tips for Success: Stay organized, enjoy learning, and remember that it's not just about deadlines but understanding concepts deeply.

- **The Balancing Act**: Juggling like a pro, finding harmony in consistency.

  - Pros: Mr./Ms. Consistent, acing everything.
  - Cons: Routine might feel limiting; challenge yourself.
  - Tips for Success: Don't stick to the usual; stretch your mind and aim higher at every opportunity.

## TIME MANAGEMENT ARTISTRY

In a world where time is a rare commodity, nailing time management is key. Here are some tips to boost productivity and make every second count. Get set to uncover the secrets of mastering time!

### Curate Your Corner; Declutter and Organize

Getting your space in order, no matter your style, is a real game-changer. It boosts your time management and productivity. Clutter?

It's a magnet for distractions, lost items, and stress. Here's why a tidy space helps your time management skills:

- **Cuts Distractions**: Messy spaces draw your attention away. A clean area helps you focus and be more productive.
- **Boosts Visibility**: When everything's in place, you find what you need quickly. No more hunting through piles of papers.
- **Eases Decision-Making**: Clutter means too many choices. Organizing simplifies daily decisions, saving mental energy for bigger tasks.
- **Sets Up Routines**: A tidy space sets the tone for your day. Have specific areas for work, study, and relaxation to switch tasks smoothly.
- **Enhances Mood**: Chaos breeds stress. A tidy space brings peace, lifts your spirits, and reduces stress.

I get it; cleaning isn't everyone's favorite hobby, but keeping your space tidy doesn't have to be a drag. Here are some quick tips to keep things neat without spending hours:

- **Start Fresh**: Declutter by getting rid of unnecessary items. Donate or toss things to create more room.
- **Categorize and Organize**: Sort your stuff into categories like books, clothes, etc., and give each category its own spot.
- **Use Storage Solutions**: Invest in shelves, drawers, or containers to keep things tidy and easy to find.
- **Filing System**: Organize important papers with folders, binders, or digital solutions for quick access.
- **Maintain Order**: Make tidying up a daily habit. Spend a few minutes each day putting things back where they belong.

Finding the right organizational system can take some trial and error, but it's worth it. An orderly space makes managing your hectic schedule much easier and boosts your well-being.

## *Prioritize: First Things First!*

Managing your time isn't just about getting organized; it's about focusing on what really matters. Here are some strategies to help you find your rhythm:

- **Use Lists**: Write down your tasks however you like—on paper, a digital tool, or an app. I prefer Google Docs with color coding for urgency.
- **ABCDE Method**: Prioritize tasks with letters from "A" (most crucial) to "E" (least crucial). This helps you focus on the important stuff.
- **Eisenhower Matrix**: Sort tasks by urgency and importance, then decide whether to tackle, schedule, delegate, or skip them.
- **Ivy Lee Method**: At the end of each day, list six key tasks for tomorrow, prioritize them, and tackle them in order. Simple and effective.
- **Do the Worst Thing First**: Knock out the toughest task early in the day. This sets a positive tone and ensures you get it done quickly.

When your to-do list is screaming "urgent," talk to your mentor. Ask questions like:

- Which projects will cause chaos if delayed?
- What are the big wins if we act on specific projects now?
- What's long term, and what needs immediate focus?

Feel free to try any of these methods or create your own system that works best for you!

*Set SMART Goals*

Think of SMART as your goal-setting cheat code. It stands for Specific, Measurable, Achievable, Relevant, and Time-bound. Let's break that down without getting all fancy.

- **Get Specific**: Instead of vague goals, be clear. Say, "Start jogging three times a week" instead of "Be more active."
- **Measure It Up**: Make goals trackable. Like a video game progress bar, you want to see movement!
- **Keep It Real**: Set doable goals. Consider your skills, time, and resources to make sensible plans.
- **Stay Relevant**: Goals should matter. Why are you doing this? Make sure it fits your life's big picture.
- **Time It Right**: Give your goals a deadline. This adds urgency and keeps you on track.

Here are tips to make your goals a reality:

- **Clear Goal**: Choose a goal that's specific. Instead of "get fit," go for "do yoga every morning."
- **Action Steps**: Break your goal into smaller tasks, like tackling one level at a time in a game—less overwhelming, more doable.
- **Track Progress**: Decide how you'll measure success. Count reps and track days—just make sure you see your wins.
- **Reality Check**: Be honest. Can you actually do this with what you have right now? If yes, you're set.
- **Relevance Check**: Ask yourself if this goal fits into your life. If not, tweak it.
- **Set a Deadline**: Give yourself a timeline. It's not about rushing, but having a finish line keeps you focused and moving forward.

SMART goals aren't rocket science; they're just a clever way to make your goals actually work.

### Run a Time Audit

Before planning your schedule, see where your time actually goes. Create a visual map of your activities—work, school, chores, commuting, social media, and free time. Break down your past week by days and hours to spot any time-wasters, like too much phone scrolling eating into study or work time (Odendahl, 2023).

- Try the AAA approach—Awareness, Arrangement, Adaptation:

  - Awareness: Keep track of your time.
  - Arrangement: Get your tasks in order.
  - Adaptation: Adjust as needed.

- Notice your energy peaks? Match high-energy tasks with those times.
- Separate high-value tasks from low-value ones and spot distractions. Maybe cut down on unnecessary email checks?

Based on your time study, adjust and redistribute your efforts for better time management.

### Time Management Techniques

Are your tasks organized but need a game plan to tackle them all day? Without one, you'll be playing catch-up. Try these time management tricks with your prioritization strategy to boost productivity!

- **Pomodoro Technique**: Set a timer for 25 minutes, work on a task until it rings, then take a short break. Repeat, and after four rounds, enjoy a longer break.

- **Time Blocking**: Divide your day into blocks for specific tasks. Use a tool like Google Calendar to stay organized and avoid multitasking.
- **Batching**: Group similar tasks and handle them together. This saves you from constantly switching gears.
- **Getting Things Done (GTD)**: Follow David Allen's workflow:

  - Capture: Write down all tasks causing stress or demanding attention.
  - Clarify: Determine if tasks are actionable, decide the next steps, and categorize them.
  - Organize: Place tasks in suitable locations, such as planners, calendars, or lists, and regularly review and update them.
  - Deal with tasks under two minutes immediately, discard nonactionable ones, and schedule future tasks. Stick to these principles for efficient task management.

Start with a weekly planning session to prioritize tasks. Stick to your plan and adjust as needed for a productivity boost!

### *Cut Back on Multitasking*

Years of brain science and recent studies say multitasking is a productivity killer. Instead of getting more done, you do less, miss important details, and need 15 minutes to refocus after distractions. Efficiency drops by 40 percent, work quality suffers, and your creativity and memory take a hit.

A University of London study found that multitasking can lower your IQ, like skipping a night's sleep. So, even if you think you're being productive, you're actually working with a dimmer bulb, costing companies money. Based on MRI scans, it messes with your brain's empathy and emotion zones. Plus, those quick wins from multitasking are just fooling you into feeling efficient (Giang, 2016).

How to tackle multitasking madness:

- Focus on one task for 20 minutes before switching. No task hopping.
- Check emails at set times, not constantly. Tame the inbox beast.
- Eliminate distractions. Turn off alerts, find a quiet spot, and declutter.
- Keep your workspace tidy. Less mess, less stress.
- Practice mindfulness. Stay present and catch yourself before you multitask.

In short, multitasking can fry your brain, but interruptions are inevitable. Just decide which interruptions are worth it and what info you really need.

### Delegate Like a Boss

Type A folks love to juggle too many tasks, thanks to their go-getter nature. But whether you're Type A or not, sharing the workload in class can boost your time management. Delegating means offloading less urgent tasks so you can tackle the big stuff. Start by deciding what to delegate, like the research for a group project. Pick someone skilled and offer guidance if needed.

### Embrace Flexibility

Life throws curveballs—extra tasks, sudden deadlines, or personal emergencies. Don't sweat what you could've done differently; forgive yourself and move on. Remember, planning is just a tool. Stay flexible, especially in a crisis. Sometimes, you need to ditch the task list and adapt, switching tasks if your focus is shot.

*Reassess and Adapt*

After a month of your new time management plan, reassess what's working and what's not. Adjust your strategy for better results. Keep practicing and tweaking as your priorities change. What worked in school might need an update for a new job. Remember, mastering time management is an ongoing process, not a one-time fix.

## TIME MASTERY FOR A HEALTHIER YOU

Taking care of yourself is key to feeling great physically, mentally, and emotionally. It involves a mix of activities that boost your health and happiness. Now, let's see how time management can help you fit self-care into your day.

*SMART Well-Being Goals*

Setting SMART health goals is a smart way to focus your efforts for better results. Here are some examples:

- **Specific**

  - General Goal: "Get healthier."
  - SMART Goal: "Limit sugary drinks to one per day, replacing the rest with water or herbal tea."

- **Measurable**

  - General Goal: "Exercise more."
  - SMART Goal: "Walk briskly for 30 minutes, 5 days a week, and track progress with a fitness app."

- **Achievable**

  - General Goal: "Lose weight."
  - SMART Goal: "Lose 10 pounds in the next 2 months by controlling portions, cutting sugary snacks, and exercising 150 minutes a week."

- **Relevant**

  - General Goal: "Improve overall health."
  - SMART Goal: "Incorporate cardio, strength training, and flexibility exercises into my weekly routine."

- **Time-Bound**

  - General Goal: "Eat more fruits and vegetables."
  - SMART Goal: "Increase daily fruit and veggie intake to five servings within the next four weeks, adding them to every meal."

Remember, these are just starting points. Tweak them to fit your needs. And always check with a healthcare professional before making big changes to your diet or exercise routine!

*Self-Care Routines*

Setting up a routine can seriously boost your ability to prioritize self-care every day. A good routine helps you manage your time, cut stress, and make room for self-care even when you're super busy. Here's how:

- **Structure and Predictability**: A routine brings order to your day, cutting down on stress and anxiety. Knowing what's next helps you feel more in control.

- **Time Allocation and Prioritization**: A routine helps you use time wisely and focus on what matters, including self-care. Scheduling self-care ensures it doesn't get sidelined.
- **Mindfulness and Intentionality**: A routine promotes mindfulness, letting you be present and make deliberate choices about your time.

Stick to your routine, even when it gets tough, and tweak it as needed to fit your changing needs and responsibilities.

### Take Breaks

Breaks aren't just nice—they're essential for your well-being and productivity. A study from the University of Illinois found that frequent breaks during a 50-minute brain-intensive task led to the highest mental stamina.

How often should you take a break? Aim for every 50–90 minutes, aligning with the 90-minute ultradian cycles discovered by the United States Army Research Institute. If 90 minutes feels too long, go for a break every 50 minutes (Patel, 2014).

How long should your breaks be? Ideally, 15–20 minutes, but longer breaks during lunch are fine. Just set a timer so you know when to start and stop. When the timer goes off, get back to work. This keeps a short break from turning into a procrastination spree. Plan your study time, too, so you stay on track and don't turn your break into a crafting session (Patel, 2014).

Tips to make your breaks count:

- **Keep Breaks Regular**: Don't wait until you're exhausted. Plan breaks throughout the day to keep your energy up.
- **Change the Scene**: Step away from your study spot to clearly separate work from relaxation. A walk in the park can make a big difference.

- **Unplug**: Reduce screen time during breaks. Your eyes and brain will thank you.
- **Chill Mindfully**: Try stress-busting activities like meditation, deep breathing, or stretching during breaks.
- **Have Fun**: Do things you enjoy—read, listen to music, or hang out with loved ones. Avoid time-suckers like social media and binge-watching.
- **Snack Smart**: Choose healthy snacks like fruits, nuts, lean proteins, and slow-release carbs. Skip sugary drinks and junk food to avoid crashes.
- **Master the Nap**: Napping is great! Set a timer for 20 minutes to stay in a light sleep stage. Short naps refresh you without messing up your nighttime sleep.

Nailing your breaks can be a stress-buster. Plan smart, chill hard, and disconnect for a refreshing reboot.

**INFO BIT#12:** Kids might nap a lot, but adults get back into it after fifty-five. Still, many of us get sleepy about 8 hours after waking up. A quick nap can refresh you and boost your alertness. A midday snooze or "power nap" brings perks: less stress, better focus, improved memory, and overall health. While we need 7–9 hours of sleep, over a third of Americans get less than 7 hours of sleep a night.

Lack of sleep can mess with your brain, causing poor judgment, slow reactions, and a higher risk of accidents. It can also lead to headaches, lower immunity, and cravings that add pounds. Over time, it might cause serious health issues like high blood pressure, diabetes, and heart disease. The urge to take an afternoon nap comes from a brain chemical called adenosine. Napping helps clear this chemical, making you feel more awake. NASA found that a 26-minute nap boosts alertness by 54 percent and job performance by 34 percent. But most experts suggest a 10–20-minute power nap for a quick refresh without feeling groggy. Longer naps, around 60–90 minutes, can be even more restorative because they let you complete a full sleep cycle.

If you wake up groggy, you might need a bit more snooze time to finish your cycle (Scott, 2023).

Tips for better naps:

- Skip caffeine after 3 p.m. to avoid sleep disruption.
- Set an alarm to keep naps short.
- Try meditation if you can't nap; it can relax you and mimic light sleep.

Happy napping!

### *Say No*

Getting comfortable with saying no can be a powerful tool for establishing healthy boundaries, safeguarding your time and energy, and creating room for what truly matters.

- Avoid overcommitting to prevent burnout and stress. Learn to say no to extra requests.
- Preserve your time and energy by declining activities that don't align with your priorities.
- Prioritize self-care by making time for activities that promote well-being. Saying no to external demands frees up space for self-care activities, whether it's pursuing hobbies or simply relaxing.
- Set clear boundaries to protect your well-being. Asserting your needs and values is the key to strengthening your personal boundaries and self-respect.
- Saying no empowers you to focus on what truly matters in your life, fostering well-being and building boundaries.

Keep in mind that your time and energy are precious resources; use them wisely.

**INFO BIT#13:** Throughout history, big shots have tried all sorts of tricks to get more done. Scan this QR code to see what Bill Gates says about managing time!

## TIME MANAGEMENT ROADBLOCKS

Time management can be a real puzzle, even for adults. As a teen juggling school, hobbies, and friends, you're sure to encounter a few tricky time traps. Here are some you might face:

### Procrastination

Procrastination: the timeless struggle of getting stuff done. Whether it's boredom, overwhelm, or just plain "meh," we've all been there. Fear of failing or chasing perfection only adds to the fun. And let's face it, who hasn't caved to the siren call of a quick mood boost? But hey, take it from Mark Twain: "Eat the Frog," which isn't about culinary adventures; it's about tackling your toughest tasks head-on.

- **Zeigarnik Effect**: Starting's the tough part, but once you're rolling, your brain nags you to keep at it. It's like your brain's way of saying, "Hey, don't forget about this!"
- **Get Moving**: Physical activity gives your brain a boost and amps up your energy. Taking a quick stroll or doing some exercise can clear your mind and make it easier to tackle that thing you've been avoiding.
- **Accountability**: Tell someone about your goal, time management tactics, and deadline—a friend, a tutor, or whoever will keep you on track.
- **Reward System**: Save your favorite tunes or fun activities for when you're tackling the boring stuff. Or treat yourself to a nice dinner once you've conquered that task.

Beat procrastination: Tackle the hard tasks first, use the Zeigarnik effect, get moving, find an accountability buddy, and treat yourself when you finish!

### Distractions

Teens often get sidetracked because their brains are still figuring out planning and focus. Smartphones and social media add to the distraction. Scrolling through social media can waste time, mess with focus, ruin sleep, and bring you down by comparing yourself to others. Managing your time keeps you organized, which is key to success and feeling good. As you grow, it's up to you to take charge of your health and life.

### Stress

Balancing everything can be stressful and hurt your performance. Good time management is key to keeping stress under control.

## CHAPTER ACTIVITIES

### Future Reflections

Picture yourself thirty years from now, looking back on how today's choices shaped your life. Feel the joy or regret based on how you managed your time. Jot down your thoughts and consider tweaking your habits for a brighter future.

### Productivity Times Survey

Find your peak productivity moments! Take a quiz, uncover your rhythm, and get tips on maximizing your energy highs. Schedule tasks smartly to match your peak times and breeze through your day!

## Questions

- **Morning Person or Night Owl?**

  a. I'm a morning person; I feel most energized and focused early on.
  b. I'm a night owl; I'm most alert and productive late at night.

- **Afternoon Slump?**

  a. I feel a bit sluggish and less focused during the afternoon.
  b. I maintain my energy and focus pretty well throughout the day.

- **Weekend Warrior?**

  a. I tackle tasks and projects on weekends.
  b. Weekends are for relaxing and recharging; I'm more productive on weekdays.

- **Breaks and Refreshers?**

  a. I enjoy short breaks to recharge during the day.
  b. I prefer to keep going without many breaks.

- **Social vs. Solitude?**

  a. I work best alone without distractions.
  b. I enjoy social environments and find them energizing.

## Results and Tips

- If you got mostly A's, you're probably a morning person! Focus on tackling tough tasks in the morning when you're

most energized. Plan meetings or study sessions to maximize
your productivity.
- If you got mostly B's, you're probably a night owl or just
steady throughout the day! Use your afternoons or evenings
for lighter tasks or things you enjoy. And don't forget to take
breaks to stay energized!

Knowing when you're at your best can make a big difference. Keep
track of your energy levels and tasks for a week, then adjust your
schedule accordingly. Simple as that!

### Elevate the Gaps

Make the most of your waiting time! Whether you're on the move or
between appointments, boost your productivity. Listen to podcasts,
read, or review your notes. Share your wins with friends and swap
ideas!

### Crush It with Automation!

Jump into the world of automation or batching, whether it's prepping
meals or sorting study stuff. Share your time-saving tricks and join
the chatter! Let's make tasks smoother and high-five our efficiency
wins while making sure they play by the rules. Ready, set, optimize!

### LIGHTBULB MOMENT

We dished out the deets on managing time, crushing goals, and
throwing in a casual "no." Now, go own that teen life like a boss—it's
all yours!

Next, we'll help you navigate money management, grasp budgeting
basics, create a spending plan, and offer advice for securing your first
job. Get ready to take charge of your financial path!

# INSPIRE NEW JOURNEYS BY SHARING YOUR REVIEW

I hope you've been enjoying this book so far! Writing it was like taking a stroll down memory lane, revisiting those years of learning my lessons the hard way, with all their twists and turns. While it's not a quick read, my aim has been to shed light on both the beautiful tulip mazes and the bumpy roads ahead. If you've found value in these pages, your feedback on Amazon would mean the world to me and to other readers facing similar struggles who could relate to your experience. Who knows? Your words might ignite a chain reaction of positive transformations! Scanning the below QR code takes you to our Amazon review page:

Let's support each other and grow together, one day, one chapter, one book at a time! Shall we?

Your Middle Eastern Bestie

# MASTERING FINANCIAL LITERACY

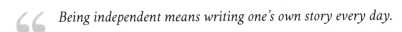

*Being independent means writing one's own story every day.*

— OM

I totally get it. I was once craving independence like crazy. Being the boss of my own life sounded amazing. But here's the catch: I had no clue what I was getting into. All I had was this big dream of being a successful, free-spirited person taking on the world.

Honestly, that vision was what kept me going, but my financial cluelessness led to some stressful money situations. For those feeling like I did, independence isn't all glamorous like in movies. It's about learning hard lessons and facing tough situations that make you stronger.

Let's break down the key milestones on your road to financial independence (Naik, 2022):

- **Age Thirteen**: Cost of Living: Learn about bills like heating, electricity, and water. Save money by turning off lights and taking showers instead of baths.

- **Age Fourteen**: Investing: Get into investing, especially if you're into cryptocurrencies from gaming. Try a stock market game online to practice without real money.
- **Age Fifteen**: Credit and Jobs: Understand debit, credit, and store cards. Learn about credit costs and Buy Now, Pay Later (BNPL) deals. Consider getting a summer job in offices, amusement parks, or restaurants. Get an ATM card for your savings account. Dreaming of your own gig someday? Start planning now.
- **Age Sixteen**: Earning and Work: If you haven't started a part-time or summer job, now's the time. Open a checking account with a debit card to learn money management before college. Cosign the account if needed due to age restrictions.
- **Age Seventeen**: Credit Reports: Learn about credit reports and your credit history. Check your report to keep things straight for future credit needs.
- **Age Eighteen**: Student Loans: If you're heading to college, understand student loans. Federal loans offer fixed rates and flexible payments, while private ones may have variable rates and fewer options. Know the real costs before diving in.

In this chapter, we're diving into money tips to boost your financial smarts. Then, we'll cover landing teen jobs and wrap up with tips for looking professional. Remember, everyone's path to independence is unique, with its own bumps and highlights. So don't stress if you haven't hit a milestone yet—it's all part of the ride.

*Chista, 2023. Artwork created using Midjourney.*

## HANDLING PERSONAL FINANCES

Let's jump into the essential world of personal finances. I know it's not as fun as the latest TikTok craze, but being money-savvy is crucial. Ignoring it won't just hurt your wallet; it might stress out your folks about the budget. Quick stats: most teens feel clueless about money, and a whopping 86 percent want to invest but don't know how. Where does their cash go? Mostly on food, fashion, and personal care—the teen essentials. Now, let's skip the fluff and dive into practical budgeting tips and money practices (Sharkey, 2022).

### *Budgeting Basics*

Think of budgeting as your financial GPS guiding you to a stable future. It's not about quick fixes but about making choices that pay off in the long run. It's like resisting that tempting marshmallow—self-discipline is key. Here's the lowdown:

- **Keep tabs on your cash flow**. Track what you earn and spend. Deduct your expenses from your income.
- **Set goals**. Decide what you're aiming for—whether it's saving for a new gadget or building an emergency fund.
- **Pick your budgeting style**. Choose a method that works for you and stick with it.
- **Keep an eye out**. Regularly check in and tweak as needed. Budgeting isn't about being a money hermit; it's about being savvy with your cash.

Budgeting isn't about hoarding money; it's about managing it wisely, knowing what comes in and goes out, and making smart choices. Plus, it helps ease financial stress.

### Get Creative: Diversify Your Hustles

When it comes to making money as a teen, don't rely on just one source.

- **Mix It Up**: Having a few income streams adds stability. Think side hustles or stashing cash in a high-interest account. Maybe try pet sitting or starting a YouTube channel.
- **Boost Your Skills**: Learn useful stuff like starting a business, web design, or digital marketing. It'll open up more doors for work.
- **Track Your Cash**: Keep tabs on where your money comes from, whether it's allowances or part-time gigs. Get the lowdown on gross vs. net pay and those sneaky taxes. Stay sharp with your cash.

### Spending: Know Your Bucks

Spending: Track Your Cash: Let's chat about your spending habits. Write down every expense, even the little ones—those daily coffees really add up! Here are some savvy spending tips:

- **Avoiding Discretionary Expenses**

  - Sort your needs (like food, transport, and school stuff) from your wants (like fun and games).
  - Don't fall for impulse buys; make a list and stick to it!
  - Before splurging, take a breather. A little waiting might save you some serious cash.

- **Plan Your Weekly Grocery Shopping**

  - Make a list before you go—no "I forgot the milk" excuses!
  - Load up on budget-friendly, healthy stuff like tuna, eggs, beans, and lentils.

- Don't shop hungry unless you want a cart full of snacks you didn't plan for.
- Price check like a pro, especially for clothes and kicks. No surprises at checkout!

Watch out for sneaky fees for various services! Don't fall victim to "fee inflation" and surprise charges that can wreak havoc on your budget.

- **Broadband and Television Fees**

  - Watch out for those sneaky fees in your cable and internet bills.
  - Push for clear prices and think about switching to streaming services.

- **Payment Apps Transfer Fees**

  - Know the lowdown on P2P payment apps' instant transfer fees.
  - Check out Zelle for free instant money moves.

- **Banking Account Fees**

  - Pick an account type that matches your wallet to avoid pesky fees.
  - Consider opening savings accounts with your checking to dodge some fees.
  - Keep an eye out for sneaky bank fees like maintenance, ATM, and overdraft charges. Aim for banks with fewer or no fees. Stick to in-network ATMs to cut costs. Be mindful of annual fees and aim to skip them. Set up alerts to dodge overdrafts and their fees. Chat with your bank about waiving fees if you occasionally go overboard.

- **Restaurant and Food Delivery Fees**

  - Watch out for those sneaky credit card fees when dining out! Try ringing up your orders directly to dodge those pesky extra charges from third-party delivery apps.

- **Car Rental Considerations**

  - Know your toll transponder fees and sign up if necessary.
  - Hold onto those rental keys tight to dodge those hefty replacement fees.

- **Airline and Hotel Fees**

  - Watch out for sneaky airline fees when you board, and don't get bamboozled by extra charges for picking your seat.
  - Before you raid that mini-bar at the hotel, make sure you're not gonna get hit with some surprise fees (Gill, 2024).

- **Share the Joy!**

  - Giving to others spreads smiles.

### Set Financial Goals

Let's chat about money goals—think of it as your financial GPS. SMART goals are like simple road signs for your wallet adventures. There is no need for fancy finance jargon. Let's break down SMART:

- **S—Specific**: Get laser-focused on your dreams. Be clear about where your money needs to go.
- **M—Measurable**: Numbers talk! Make your goals measurable, like hitting a savings target or paying off a specific amount.

- **A—Achievable**: Dream big but keep it real. Goals should be challenging yet doable, like finding that sweet spot between ambition and reality.
- **R—Relevant**: Money's got a job. Make sure your goals line up with what really matters to you, giving your financial journey some purpose.
- **T—Time-Bound**: Set a date! It's like giving your goals a deadline. This adds a beat to your money journey, making it less of a marathon and more of a catchy tune.

In a nutshell, SMART financial goals keep you on track without losing your mind. Here's the lowdown:

- **Break It Down**: Don't try to climb Everest in one leap. Slice those big goals into bite-sized bits. Want a $1,000 vacation? That's just $83 a month. Easy peasy!
- **Stay Flexible**: Life throws curveballs, so be ready to bend your goals. Flexibility is key to financial victory.
- **Check Progress Often**: Keep an eye on your *goal-o-meter*. Regular checks keep you in line and let you tweak if needed.
- **Celebrate Small Wins**: Give yourself a high five for every little victory. You earned it!

Setting goals doesn't have to be boring. Keep it real, keep it fun, and watch your financial dreams take flight!

### Create a Budget Plan

Think of budgeting as planning your financial home. You decide where your money goes—essentials, savings, and fun stuff. Here's the lowdown:

- **Live within Your Means**

    o Don't splurge your entire paycheck; spend less than you earn.
    o Share a place, cook at home, and find cheap hobbies.

- **Manage Your Income Wisely**

    o Use apps or spreadsheets to track spending.
    o Review and tweak your budget regularly.

Explore various budgeting strategies to find your financial sweet spot:

- **The 50/20/30 Trick**: Split 50 percent for needs, 20 percent for savings, and 30 percent for discretionary spending or fun stuff.
- **Pay Yourself First**: Put some money into savings right when you get paid. Pay bills next, then use the rest however you like.
- **Envelope Budgeting**: Put money in envelopes for different categories. When one's empty, no more spending there until next month. Leftover cash can be used later, changed, or saved.

Budgeting keeps your finances in check and steers you toward stability.

### Building Your Money Game Plan

Taxes might not be on your radar now, but understanding the basics early on sets you up for financial adulthood. Plus, you could score a refund! Let's break down how to allocate the money in your wallet:

1. **Tax**: That money you make from your summer or part-time gig? Not all of it sticks around. Taxes take a slice, but it's worth it for money smarts. Here's the scoop:

- Income Tax: It's the government's cut from your paycheck or tips. You can't dodge this one!
- Payroll Tax: That chunk missing from your paycheck? That's Social Security and Medicare taking a nibble.
- Sales Tax: Shopping? Sales tax varies by state and adds a bit to what you pay for goods and services.
- Why It Matters: Knowing tax basics now is like a backstage pass to how your country runs!

2. **Debt Reduction:** Tackle those debts, especially those with high interest rates, to boost your financial game. Get the hang of responsible borrowing and building credit.

   - Good vs. Bad Debt: Some debts help, like student loans, while others do not so much.
   - Card Choices: Keep it simple with a debit card.
   - Build Credit: A good score is like a golden ticket for future perks.

3. **Emergency Fund**: Keep cash for life's surprises like unexpected bills or sudden repairs—your financial safety net.
4. **Savings**: Saving is like your own personal "marshmallow test"— saying no to instant rewards for bigger payoffs down the road. Starting to save early sets you up for stability and opens up future possibilities.
5. **Investments**: Dip your toes into the world of growing wealth— think stocks and retirement accounts. Investing might sound fancy, but it's just putting your money where it can grow and benefit you later. Keep it simple, mix things up, and let your money hustle for your dreams.

   - Investing 101: Start early, and time becomes your money-making buddy. No need to overcomplicate; even teens can ride the investment wave with a bit of know-how.

- Mix It Up: Make your money work for you! Consider investing in stocks and bonds for bigger returns than a regular savings account. Tailor it to your goals, like saving for college or buying your dream home.

6. **Insurance**: From health to life and property, insurance keeps you shielded from life's curveballs.
7. **Income Growth**: Boost your income game by acquiring new skills and seizing those golden career opportunities.
8. **Retirement Realities**: Golden Years Plan: Start saving early for retirement. While a teen might not qualify for a 401(k), exploring an individual retirement plan (IRA) sets the stage for future financial stability.
9. **Continuous Learning**: Stay in the know with ongoing financial education. Informed decisions pave the way to financial success.

### Some Points to Keep in Mind

Stay protected with these smart tips:

- **Check Your Statements**: Regularly review your credit card statements to spot and stop any suspicious activity.
- **Secure Your Documents**: Store important papers safely. Shred or tear them up before disposal to protect your information.
- **Use Antivirus Software**: Install and update antivirus programs to guard against online threats.
  - Strengthen Your Passwords: Create strong, unique passwords for each account to keep them secure.
  - Be Resourceful: Research and seek advice from experts when you need it.

*Teenage Job Seeking Guidance*

Looking for a job as a teenager can feel overwhelming. You need to figure out what kind of job you're interested in, what you're good at, and where you'd like to work. Here are some helpful tips to get you started:

- Find what you enjoy doing to start your job search. What activities make you happy? This can help you find jobs you'll like more.
- Talk to friends and family before applying. They might know about job openings you haven't thought of. Ask about their work and what they like about it.
- Search for jobs online on sites like Indeed or Monster. But be careful of strange job offers. Stick to well-known sites to avoid weird situations. Keep your job hunt safe and simple.
- Check out local businesses you like. They might be hiring. Your dream job could be close by.
- Don't forget about your school's career center. They might have job leads or events to help you meet potential employers. Your school could help you find your first job.

And remember, stay true to yourself as you navigate this journey. Balancing professionalism with your personality can make you stand out and land you the perfect job.

*Rocking Your First Job*

When you're going for a job, your future boss might want to chat with you to get to know you better. They might ask for a resume or cover letter, so make sure you have those ready. Here are some tips for your first meeting or interview with the employer:

*Chista, 2023. Artwork created using Midjourney.*

- **Customize Your Docs**: Tailor your resume and cover letter for each job. Avoid the one-size-fits-all approach—show you're really interested in the job.
- **Practice for the Interview**: Get familiar with common interview questions. Practice your responses so you can go into the interview feeling confident.
- **Dress Nicely**: Dress a bit more formal for interviews. It shows you're serious about the job and ready to work.
- **Stay Positive**: Bring a positive attitude to the interview. Show you're a hard worker and excited about potentially joining their team.

Congrats on landing the job! Now, let's make sure you excel with these laid-back tips.

- **Be On Time**: Always arrive punctually and don't skip any workdays.
- **Be Ready to Learn**: Embrace the learning process, ask questions, and show you're committed to doing a good job.
- **Be a Team Player**: Get along with your coworkers and help out when needed to build good relationships.
- **Stay Positive**: Maintain a positive attitude and enthusiasm for your work. This makes you enjoyable to work with and noticeable to your boss.

Scoring a job as a teen can be tough, but it's a cool opportunity to learn and grow.

## CHAPTER ACTIVITIES

### *Earning Wings Challenge*

Try out different ways to make money, and then share your experience with your peers.

### *Smart Spending Simulation*

Try tracking your spending for a week and talking about it together. Share the challenges and what you learned, stressing how important it is to spend wisely.

### *Budgeting App Exploration*

Check out different budgeting apps together. Talk about what they can do, what's good about them, and what's not so great. Let everyone pick the one they like best.

### *Delayed Gratification Exercise*

Talk about times when waiting for a better deal or saving up for something nicer paid off. Chat about the idea of waiting for what you really want and have the girls share their stories.

### *Learning from Financial Mistakes*

Share your money mishaps and talk about what you learned from them. Stress how important it is to grow from our slip-ups.

## LIGHTBULB MOMENT

Mastering personal finances as a teen lays the groundwork for life-long financial stability. By learning practical budgeting, different ways to earn money, and smart spending habits, you're preparing for a secure and stress-free financial future. Have you ever thought about how dreams turn into careers? Get ready for the next part, where we'll discuss dreaming big, deciding what you want, and planning your next steps.

# DREAM, DISCOVER, DECIDE

*The path from dreams to success does exist. May you have the vision to find it, the courage to get on to it, and the perseverance to follow it.*

— KALPANA CHAWLA

Since childhood, making others happy has always been my thing. Growing up with three physician family members—my dad and two siblings—I always perceived healthcare-related jobs as the ultimate form of helping others. So, I chose to become a pharmacist, which opened up a world of diverse career opportunities. Luckily, despite having no access to the plethora of resources available to kids today, I have no regrets about my decision. What seemed daunting for many my age felt like a natural choice, guided by my self-awareness and years of observation.

Today, students face tough job competition and need many skills, making the job market overwhelming. However, choosing a job should still be about providing for yourself and enjoying what you do. With all the information and choices available, focus on what truly makes you happy. After all, a high salary won't make you happy if you dislike your job.

Experts suggest thinking about career plans early. Many high school grads wish they'd started sooner. Middle school offers more time to explore different careers and take relevant classes and activities. Starting early gives you hope and direction, making your goals seem achievable. If your first goal doesn't work out, you can try something else. Knowing your main path and backup plans boosts confidence and puts you ahead.

Even if schools don't offer career classes, you can still learn a lot on your own with some time and effort. Let's get started with the basics!

## SELF-REFLECT

Since you spend most of your time at work, choose a job that makes you happy. Start by exploring different aspects of yourself to help make this important decision.

- **Self-Assessment**: Identify what excites you. Think about hobbies and experiences that bring you joy, as they can point to your passions.
- **Find Your Values**: Determine what matters most to you. Consider the impact you want to have, whether it's through creativity, teamwork, making a difference, or learning. Knowing your values helps match your career to your beliefs.
- **Personality Check**: Reflect on your work style and personality. Do you prefer a fast-paced environment or structure? Do you enjoy working with people, numbers, things, or ideas? Understanding your personality helps you find a suitable job.
- **Skills Inventory**: List your strengths, whether natural or learned. Consider skills from school, work, or life experiences, including important soft skills like communication, leadership, teamwork, and adaptability. The

"Intrinsic Value Vault" chapter activity at the end of Chapter 1 can be a starting point.

Use useful assessments and ask teachers, mentors, or parents for advice. This will give you a better idea of your goals. If you're still uncertain about your career path, it's okay! The next step is to explore different options.

DREAM

*Chista, 2023. Artwork created using Midjourney.*

Dream big, follow your passions, and visualize your career goals—this isn't silly; it's essential for success. Vision links the present to the future and gives purpose to our efforts. Without it, we may lose our way and opt for easy routes to avoid discomfort. Our destiny is shaped by choices, not chance, and starts with a strong desire. Vision requires understanding and can't be handed to us. It gives purpose to our sacrifices, making them meaningful. Life has stages, and trying to skip them will catch up with us.

Here's why developing a clear vision regularly is beneficial:

- Your brain reacts as if you've already succeeded, boosting your motivation and performance. This releases dopamine, making you feel good and reinforcing positive habits.
- It helps make your goals more achievable because you act in

ways that support them. It also makes you happier by focusing on successes rather than failures.

- As a leader, it helps you set clear goals and inspire and encourage your team, improving overall performance and morale.
- It makes you more resilient, better at handling problems, and encourages creative thinking. It lessens stress and anxiety, helping you bounce back from tough times.

Vision boards can help clarify goals and keep you focused.

**INFO BIT#14:** Growing a vision has always been the most fundamental step toward accomplishing major feats throughout history. Historical figures knew the power of vision.

- Life is one big road with lots of signs. So when you're riding through the ruts, don't complicate your mind. Flee from hate, mischief, and jealousy. Don't bury your thoughts; put your vision into reality. — Bob Marley, "Wake Up and Live"
- The only thing worse than being blind is having sight but no vision. — Helen Keller
- In order to carry a positive action, we must develop here a positive vision. — Dalai Lama
- The path from dreams to success does exist. May you have the vision to find it, the courage to get on to it, and the perseverance to follow it. — Kalpana Chawla
- Vision without action is merely a dream. Action without vision just passes the time. Vision with action can change the world. — Joel A. Barker
- Vision is the art of seeing what is invisible to others. — Jonathan Swift

## DISCOVER

Research and discovery are where things really heat up! Finding careers that fit your dreams takes some serious thought and self-reflection, along with plenty of hands-on exploration and trial and error. To make the most of what you've got (Texas OnCourse, 2021):

- **Explore:** Don't miss out on school events like career fairs and assessments. Explore resources like CareerOneStop, The Forage, the Department of Labor, and MyCareerTech to dig into different careers.

  - Wages: See what you could earn at the start and factor in any student loans.
  - Education and Licenses: Check what you need to study and any certifications, considering costs and location.
  - Job Outlook: Look into the future of your chosen field.
  - Demographics: Check out who usually works in the field and how it affects things like pay and location.
  - Job Availability: Figure out how many job openings there are in the field.
  - Tasks and Skills: Get a feel for what you'll do and what skills you'll need.

- **Experiment**: Talk to people who work in those jobs to gain firsthand experience; volunteer, intern, or visit workplaces. You can also join summer camps or workshops to learn more. Look for apprenticeship programs or part-time jobs to get hands-on experience.
- **Networking and Mentorship**: Get advice from career counselors, mentors, or professionals in the fields you're interested in. Their tips, guidance, and connections can help shape your career decisions and create opportunities for growth and happiness (Perry, 2023).

Stay curious and keep exploring. Your future job is waiting for you, and if you have a clear goal and work hard, you can achieve it. If you're not sure what you want to do yet, try a career cluster inventory. It helps you find jobs that match your interests by grouping similar ones together. You might find options like audio engineering or graphic design if you like music. Check out these inventories on high school, college, and state education websites to discover new opportunities.

DECIDE

*Chista, 2023. Artwork created using Midjourney.*

Once you've chosen a couple of careers and received some good advice, here's what to do next:

- Set clear personal and professional goals to stay focused and motivated while pursuing the education and skills for your chosen career.
- Consider different ways to enter your career, like college, training programs, or on-the-job learning.

Keep in mind that your path can open up lots of doors. If your interests shift, you can use what you've learned in other areas. Don't stress if you're not starting at the top—everyone's journey is unique, and there are plenty of ways to climb the ladder as you go.

**INFO BIT#15:** Self-reflection is essential for career success and personal growth. Regularly take time to assess yourself and identify areas for improvement in your work and surroundings. Focus on what you can control and work on those areas, continually reflecting on your progress. Here are some examples of how self-reflection on your values, interests, strengths, past challenges, achievements, and professional relationships can support your development:

- Increases self-awareness, which is vital for leadership and career growth.
- Improves decision-making by clarifying motivations and outcomes.
- Enhances creativity and problem-solving, which is important for career advancement.
- Reduces stress by helping process experiences and develop coping strategies.
- Keeps you focused on career goals and minimizes distractions.
- Builds resilience, aiding recovery from setbacks.
- Helps adapt to career changes by identifying strengths and weaknesses.
- Boosts motivation and commitment to career goals.
- Enhances emotional intelligence, improving relationships and leadership.
- Helps prioritize tasks and eliminate time-wasters.
- Promotes a healthier work-life balance.
- Improves retention and application of new skills at work.
- Increases job satisfaction.
- Helps manage emotions and reduce workplace burnout.
- Improves networking skills.

Scan the QR code below to learn more about self-development through reflective practice. This method helps you let go of your ego and become more mature and self-aware.

## CHAPTER ACTIVITIES

### *Extracurricular Explorer*

a. Explore online and ask people you know to find clubs or groups nearby that share your interests.

b. Watch out for any upcoming events or meetings. Choose a couple of clubs to check out in person. Go to one of their meetings or events to see if you like it.

c. Once you've been doing an after-school activity for a while, think about what you've gained from it. What did you learn? How has it made you grow as a person and in your skills?

d. Think about what makes you happy. What do you like doing? Write down some things you might enjoy doing outside of school or work.

e. Look online and ask people to find clubs or groups nearby that are into what you enjoy. Watch for any events or meetings they have coming up.

f. Pick a club to visit. Go to one of their meetings or events to see if you like it.

g. After being involved for a while, reflect on your experience. What have you learned? How has it helped you grow personally and professionally?

### Skill Builder Challenge

a. Choose something you want to get better at, whether it's for your job or just because you're curious.

b. Decide what you want to achieve with this skill. How will you know you're getting better or track your progress?

c. Find tools to help you learn. Look online for tutorials, books, classes, or workshops.

d. Make a plan to practice regularly. Set aside time each week to work on it and keep track of how you're doing.

e. Keep checking on your progress and change your goals and methods if you need to. Don't be afraid to try new things or ask for help from others.

### SMART Goal Setter

a. Think about what you want to achieve in your career, whether it's short term or long term. Pick something that excites you and seems doable.

b. Make your goals SMART: specific, measurable, achievable, relevant, and time-bound. Break them down into smaller tasks so you can stay focused.

c. How will you make it all happen? Come up with a plan. Whether it's studying, practicing, or learning, start taking steps toward your goal. Every little thing you do counts.

d. Share your goal with someone who can support you, like a friend or family member.

e. Keep track of your progress and celebrate each milestone you reach. Every step forward is a win.

f. Remember, plans can change, and that's okay! Stay flexible and adjust your goals as needed.

## Community Impact

a. Brainstorm volunteer opportunities that match your interests, values, and career goals. Think about causes or groups you care about and see how you can get involved.

b. Check out local nonprofits, community groups, or volunteer programs that align with your interests. Contact them to learn about volunteer opportunities, requirements, and how to get started.

c. Evaluate the volunteer options you find. Consider location, time commitment, and how they align with your goals. Choose one or more that feels right for you.

d. Make a plan for your volunteer activities. Set goals for your involvement, create a schedule, and decide how to best use your time and skills.

e. Reflect on the impact of your volunteering and what you've learned. Use this to plan your own "Power of One" project—a cool idea you can lead in your community to make things better.

## LIGHTBULB MOMENT

By reflecting on yourself, dreaming, exploring, and making decisions, you're setting yourself up for success! This leads to less stress, clearer goals, and more focused time on what really matters. In our next chapter on neuroplasticity, you'll learn practical ways to enhance your brainpower and reach your full potential. We'll cover techniques like challenging your thoughts and playing brain games to help reshape your brain for success. Stay tuned for the final chapter!

# NEUROPLASTICITY—REWIRING FOR SUCCESS

 *The illiterate of the 21st century will not be those who cannot read and write, but those who cannot learn, unlearn, and relearn.*

— ALVIN TOFFLER

I n life, one thing is for sure: learning never stops. From plants to critters, picking up new info is key to survival. They adjust, upgrade, and roll with the changes. It's all about constant learning, making evolution the true champ in keeping species kicking in this crazy world.

Like plants and critters, we humans are always learning and growing, whether it's from life lessons or professional gigs. But what makes us unique is our knack for active learning, which is our brain's incredible feature called neuroplasticity. Some pros see it as the brain's flexibility to adapt and learn, while others see it as its power to grow, heal, and bounce back.

Back in the day, folks thought once you hit adulthood, your brain was locked in. It turns out that our brains can form new connections and reorganize based on our activities, learning, or even injuries. This ability, called neuroplasticity, allows our brains to adapt and change over time. It's like our brains are flexible, not fixed. Each time we do something or remember something, it's like creating new pathways that make it easier for signals to travel.

### Transforming Challenges into Opportunities

At about three pounds, the human brain might not seem huge compared to our body, which is just 2 percent of our mass. But don't underestimate it—this powerhouse is a real energy muncher, gobbling up 25 percent of our daily intake. All thanks to those busy neurons, constantly buzzing, sending signals, chatting, and keeping those crucial connections intact.

Exercising our brain, like working out at the gym, offers many benefits. It improves our mental flexibility, emotional control, healing speed, and adaptability. By questioning our beliefs, exploring complex ideas, and accepting new viewpoints, we can become more resilient and creative. This mental rewiring makes us more positive and better equipped to handle challenges.

Let's find out how to make the most out of this incredible skill.

### How to Flex Your Mental Muscles

To tap into neuroplasticity, just adjust your mindset and take action. Whether you're on your own, with a team, or getting advice, here's what you need:

- **Practice ARRR**

    - Acknowledge: Watch out for negative thoughts and see how they mess with your mood, productivity, and energy.
    - Reframe: Turn those negative thoughts upside down and find a silver lining in every cloud!

- ○ Refocus: Flip the switch to the positive side to keep stress at bay and strategize your next steps like a pro.
- ○ Recognize: Watch out for those sneaky negative thoughts that throw you off track and swap them out for some positive vibes. Keep practicing, and soon it'll become second nature.

*Chista, 2023. Artwork created using Midjourney.*

- **Stay curious.** Question "why" and "how" to really get what's going on.
- **Stay flexible**. Stay open to changing your mind as new info pops up.
- **Set goals.** Craft a roadmap for learning with doable goals to level up your skills.
- **Hard work pays off.** Get this: putting in effort is key to your learning journey. Spend some time and energy on your goals, and boom! You'll unlock your full potential. Easy peasy!
- **See challenges as opportunities.** See setbacks as opportunities to grow, not roadblocks. Every challenge is a chance to learn and expand your skills.
- **Mistakes are okay.** Embrace mistakes—they're just stepping stones to learning! Adopt a growth mindset that treasures errors as lessons for future success.
- **Keep pushing**. Keep pushing through tough times with determination. Each setback is just a step closer to a comeback. Persistence pays off, always.

- **Learn from others**. Let their success fuel your fire. If they can do it, you can too! Let their wins inspire your own journey of growth.
- **Embrace growth**. See your potential; stay open to change to boost neuroplasticity.

Besides shifting your perspective, these simple steps tap into the power of neuroplasticity:

- **Read widely**. Reading improves your mind, vocabulary, communication, and analytical skills. Explore various books, articles, and websites beyond your usual interests to broaden your knowledge. Classics like *Oliver Twist* and *Pride and Prejudice* also offer valuable insights.
- **Learn new things**. Engaging in new activities and skills enhances neuroplasticity and boosts your mood. Embrace a growth mindset by exploring online courses and workshops to stay updated in your field. Groups like FCCLA provide support and opportunities if you're interested in family-support careers.
- **Challenge yourself**. Try using your non-dominant hand, learn a new language or instrument, paint, code, or solve puzzles. These activities boost brainpower and promote neuroplasticity.
- **Play brain games**. When it starts feeling too comfy, shake things up and push your limits. Try memory exercises, Sudoku, word puzzles, and problem-solving challenges. I'm a fan of escape rooms—they're a race against time that boosts quick thinking and problem-solving skills. What feels like playtime can actually be a brain-boosting session!
- **Socialize with intelligent people**. Surround yourself with intellectually stimulating individuals to keep your mind sharp.
- **Stay healthy**. Getting enough rest, managing stress, and relaxation are essential for a sharp brain. Fuel up with brain-boosting foods like walnuts and fatty fish such as tuna,

mackerel, and salmon. Studies, such as Harvard's "Nutritional Psychiatry: Your Brain on Food," highlight the importance of nutrition for brain health. Omega-3s can provide an extra mental boost.

- **Practice mindfulness**. It improves focus and attention, and it may even help keep your brain sharp as you age. Studies suggest that meditation can alter parts of your brain linked to sensing, thinking, and feeling, potentially fighting off age-related changes in brain structure.

- **Keep a journal**. It turns out that I am not the only one who believes journaling works wonders. What Einstein, Isaac Newton, and Thomas Jefferson had in common was that they all kept journals. Whether you're jotting down notes or working out ideas, journaling allows you to put your thoughts on paper. Making it a habit helps you delve deeper into your thoughts and sharpen your thinking.

Remember, intelligence is not just genetic; it's also about training your brain to work better. Be patient and stick to routines that enhance intelligence, and your mind will improve over time.

### Shaping a Brighter Future

Neuroplasticity is a great tool for personal growth and happiness. While we all enjoy our comfort zones because they're safe, changing habits and learning new things can be challenging. If you're aiming to improve your life, good for you! By being open-minded and taking deliberate actions, we can create a better future. This isn't just science; it's a useful tool for today and the future. Lifelong learning isn't just about passing tests or getting dream jobs; it's about becoming the best version of ourselves. In our ever-changing world, lifelong learners are prepared for anything that comes their way.

## CHAPTER ACTIVITIES

### *Neuroplasticity Challenge*

Try activities that take you out of your comfort zone, like using your non-dominant hand for writing or brushing your teeth. Notice how it feels and how much effort it takes. Share your experience with friends or family, and discuss the challenges and surprises you faced.

### *Growth Mindset Book Club*

Start a Growth Mindset Book Club and invite your friends who love to read. Enjoy inspiring books that spark curiosity and lively discussions. From uplifting stories to empowering self-help books, explore the wonders of neuroplasticity together and support each other in this journey of self-discovery.

### *Brain Games Bonanza*

Host a brain games party where everyone can enjoy memory challenges like Sudoku, word puzzles, and brain teasers. It's fun and helps keep your mind sharp. Share your favorite game with a friend and see who gets the highest score!

### *Brainy Bites Culinary*

Add brain-boosting foods like walnuts, fatty fish, and leafy greens to your meals. Try out new recipes and share them with friends or family. Talk about why good nutrition is important for brain health and come up with ideas to make better food choices together.

*Mindful Meditation Meetup*

Host a mindfulness session focused on meditation techniques to improve focus, attention, and brain health. Regular mindfulness practice can enhance your brain's performance and support emotional well-being.

## LIGHTBULB MOMENT

We talked about how our brains can work better only when we want them to, thanks to their power of neuroplasticity. We also discussed ways to make the most of this trait by shifting our mindset, trying new challenges, and taking care of ourselves. It's all about keeping the learning going to stay sharp, emotionally balanced, and resilient. And guess what? You've made it through this substantial book. Now, let's head to the conclusion to tie up loose ends and unveil the broader perspective.

# CONCLUSION

If you've made it this far without skipping, give yourself a pat on the back and a little celebration dance for starting this journey toward being YOU! Remember:

- You are as special as the universe. Own your uniqueness and let it light your way.
- Growing up can be messy, but it is a blessing. Embrace the changes; they're shaping you into who you're meant to be.
- Live a meaningful life by doing what lines up with your values and face challenges like a champ for lasting fulfillment.
- Dealing with social changes is like learning a new dance. Stay true to yourself and set boundaries to find your own groove.
- On the road from hurt to healing, understanding and compassion pave the way to respect and good vibes.
- Rocking time management is all about seizing life's little moments and keeping your priorities straight. Pick what counts, and hey, it's never too late!
- Being money-wise is your ticket to a future where you're the boss, not the bills.

- Turning dreams into action takes a journey of setting your purpose and self-discovery.
- In a world that's always changing, our adaptability is our greatest asset. Let's stay open to new ideas and keep on learning.

Don't sweat it if you're not feeling like Ms. Confidence just yet—that perfect version of yourself is never going to exist! Changing habits takes time, practice, and consistency. We've all got our quirks that tag along. As we tackle old habits, new challenges pop up alongside our new roles. Life is a rollercoaster, so stay open to learning and relearning. Goals keep us on track, but don't forget to enjoy the journey. It's about the ride, not just the destination!

Last but not least, don't let life's occasional bitterness take away your spark. Keep it on to outshine the pain and doubt.

# FINAL WORDS; NEW BEGINNINGS

Thank you for trusting me to walk you through some major life lessons. Now it's your turn to take the reins and put our conversations into action every day. If you haven't found the time to write a review yet, now is the perfect moment. Your feedback on Amazon would be incredibly valuable, especially to others who are facing similar struggles and might benefit from your insights. It's a small way to give back and potentially make a big difference in someone's life.

Also, scan the code below to access a list of useful hotlines and resources on topics such as mental health, positive body image, STEM, leadership, and empowerment.

*Supplements- The Grand Synopsis*

The books within the **Teen Life Lit Series** empower teens with independence, offering essential insights and guidance. Covering everything from managing finances and handling the home alone to dealing with boredom, these books equip young adults with the knowledge and skills needed to navigate adulthood confidently and effectively.

Make sure you subscribe to our website for early access to upcoming book titles from **Teen Life Lit Series** and other series. Why stick with just today's knowledge when you can see what's next? Let's explore and learn together!

*bit.ly/The-Grand-Synopsis*

# REFERENCES

## DECLARATION OF GENERATIVE AI AND AI-ASSISTED TECHNOLOGIES IN THE WRITING PROCESS

During the preparation of this work, the author used ChatGPT to assist in editing the manuscript. After utilizing this tool, the author reviewed and edited the content as needed and takes full responsibility for the final content of the publication.

## REFERENCES

"Best Poems | The Famous Poems Encyclopedia," n.d. https://www.best-poems.net.

"Dasht-e Lut." In *Wikipedia*, May 14, 2024. https://en.wikipedia.org/w/index.php?title=Dasht-e_Lut&oldid=1223805776.

"Physical Activity Guidelines for Americans." U.S. Department of Health and Human Services, n.d. https://health.gov/sites/default/files/2019-09/Physical_Activity_Guidelines_2nd_edition.pdf.

"Teaching Your Child Healthy Nail Care." ADD: American Academy of Dermatology Association, n.d. https://www.aad.org/public/everyday-care/nail-care-secrets/basics/nail-care.

"Time Management Tips for College Students." *ROAM Student Living* (blog), November 16, 2021. https://liveatroam.com/time-management-tips-for-college-students/.

"Understanding the New Vision for Career Development: The Role of Family." NCWD, n.d. https://capeyouth.org/wp-content/uploads/sites/9/2022/03/1.-Understanding-the-New-Vision-for-Career.pdf.

"You Are Not a Drop in the Ocean, You Are the Ocean in a Drop.," n.d. https://www.selfimprovementdailytips.com/podcast/you-are-not-a-drop-in-the-ocean-you-are-the-ocean-in-a-drop.

AAD: American Academy of Dermatology Association. "How to Clean Your Makeup Brushes," n.d. https://www.aad.org/public/everyday-care/skin-care-secrets/routine/clean-your-makeup-brushes.

ACIO. "The Correct Sitting Posture While Studying." *ALLEN Overseas* (blog), November 24, 2023. https://www.allenoverseas.com/blog/the-correct-sitting-posture-while-studying/.

ADAA: Anxiety and Depression Association of America. "Anxiety Disorders - Facts & Statistics," n.d. https://adaa.org/understanding-anxiety/facts-statistics.

Allen, Brittany, and Katy Miller. "Physical Development in Girls: What to Expect During Puberty." HealthyChildren.org, June 4, 2019. https://www.healthychildren.org/English/ages-stages/gradeschool/puberty/Pages/Physical-Development-Girls-What-to-Expect.aspx.

Alumni, Club Stories. "Career Advice for Teens: Top 10 Tips From Professionals in the Workforce." Boys & Girls Clubs of America, n.d. https://www.bgca.org/news-stories/2023/December/career-advice-for-teens-from-adults/.

Ashley. "5 Ways to Become Better At Delaying Gratification (Why It Matters)." *Tracking Happiness* (blog), November 25, 2022. https://www.trackinghappiness.com/how-to-delay-gratification/.

Atchley, Paul. "You Can't Multitask, So Stop Trying." *Harvard Business Review*, December 21, 2010. https://hbr.org/2010/12/you-cant-multi-task-so-stop-tr.

Australian Human Rights Commission. "What Is Bullying?" n.d. https://humanrights.gov.au/our-work/commission-general/what-bullying.

A-Z Quotes. "TOP 25 THRIVE QUOTES (of 979)," n.d. https://www.azquotes.com/tag/thrive.

Baker, Glen and Joya. "How to Practice Delayed Gratification." Glen and Joya Baker™, March 1, 2023. https://glenandjoyabaker.com/practice-delayed-gratification/.

Basmo. "How to Exercise While Reading a Book." Basmo, November 4, 2022. https://basmo.app/exercise-while-reading-a-book/.

Baumgartner, Michelle. "Getting Better at Delaying Gratification." Study.com, December 2019. https://study.com/blog/getting-better-at-delaying-gratification.html.

Belyh, Anastasia. "52 Inspirational (And Actionable) Time Management Quotes." *FounderJar* (blog), December 21, 2022. https://www.founderjar.com/time-management-quotes/.

Birt, Jamie. "Hard Skills vs. Soft Skills: What's the Difference?" Indeed, May 31, 2024. https://www.indeed.com/career-advice/resumes-cover-letters/hard-skills-vs-soft-skills.

Bodnar, Janet. "Financial Milestones for Kids." Kiplinger, February 13, 2008. https://www.kiplinger.com/article/saving/t065-c002-s001-financial-milestones-for-kids.html.

Bouchrika, Imed. "50 Current Student Stress Statistics: 2024 Data, Analysis & Predictions." Research.com, April 17, 2024. https://research.com/education/student-stress-statistics.

Bowles, Michelle. "7 Exercises To Do While Reading a Book." What Is That Book About, May 11, 2022. https://www.whatisthatbookabout.com/thoughtsonlit/2022/5/11/7-exercises-to-do-while-reading-a-book.

Brainscape Academy. "How and When to Take Study Breaks for Optimal Learning," October 29, 2020. https://www.brainscape.com/academy/when-take-study-breaks/.

Brainy Quote. "Top 10 Vision Quotes," n.d. https://www.brainyquote.com/lists/topics/top-10-vision-quotes.

British Heart Foundation. "8 Top Tips for Portion Control," n.d. https://www.bhf.org.uk/informationsupport/heart-matters-magazine/nutrition/weight/perfect-portions/top-tips-for-portion-control.

Burga, Solcyré. "Are Dating Apps Doing Enough to Keep You Safe?" TIME, February 17, 2023. https://time.com/6256395/dating-app-safety-tips/.

Cadman, Bethany. "Ingrown Pubic Hair: Treatment and Prevention." MedicalNewsToday, September 26, 2018. https://www.medicalnewstoday.com/arti cles/323182.

Cambridge Dictionary. "Time Management," June 5, 2024. https://dictionary. cambridge.org/us/dictionary/english/time-management.

CDC Healthy Schools. "Physical Activity Guidelines for School-Aged Children and Adolescents," August 11, 2022. https://www.cdc.gov/healthyschools/physicalactiv ity/guidelines.htm.

CDC. "Healthy Habits: Menstrual Hygiene." Water, Sanitation, and Environmentally Related Hygiene (WASH), May 7, 2024. https://www.cdc.gov/hygiene/about/ menstrual-hygiene.html.

CDC. "U.S. Teen Girls Experiencing Increased Sadness and Violence." Centers for Disease Control and Prevention, February 13, 2023. https://www.cdc.gov/media/ releases/2023/p0213-yrbs.html.

ChatterHigh. "The Complete Guide to Career Exploration: For Teens and Their Teachers," n.d. https://resources.chatterhigh.com/career-exploration-guide.

Chokrane, Charlotte Owen, Naomi Pike, Boutayna. "How To Measure Your Bra Size." Vogue, July 1, 2022. https://www.vogue.com/article/how-to-measure-for-a-bra.

Clifton, Tamara. "Exercise for Teenagers: How Much They Need, and How to Fit It In." Healthline, April 13, 2022. https://www.healthline.com/health/fitness/exercise-for-teenagers.

CollegiateParent. "Career Exploration for High School Students — 3 Steps to Follow - CollegiateParent," August 17, 2020. https://www.collegiateparent.com/high-school/ career-exploration-in-high-school/.

Cope, Sean. "18 Effective Time Management Strategies and Techniques." Upwork, April 1, 2021. https://www.upwork.com/resources/time-management-strategies.

Coursera Staff. "What Is Time Management? 6 Strategies to Better Manage Your Time." Coursera, November 29, 2023. https://www.coursera.org/articles/time-manage ment.

CPA, Echo Huang, CFA, CFP®. "10 Money Management Tips for Teens." Echo Wealth Management, March 29, 2018. https://www.echowealthmanagement.com/blog/10-money-management-tips-teens.

Cunningham, Dr Diana. "Rumi On Moving Through Grief: From Anger to Depression to Love." Medium (blog), February 28, 2020. https://dianacunningham62.medium. com/rumi-on-moving-through-grief-from-anger-to-depression-to-love-3653773a056a.

D'Amico, Pat. "Here's How Journaling Can Benefit Teens." Paradigm Treatment Center, January 11, 2018. https://paradigmtreatment.com/journaling-benefit-teens/.

Davis, Jennifer E. "Multitasking and How It Affects Your Brain Health | Lifespan." Lifespan, January 26, 2023. https://www.lifespan.org/lifespan-living/multitasking-and-how-it-affects-your-brain-health.

Davis, Josh. "How (And Why) To Master The Habit Of Delaying Gratification." Fast Company, January 17, 2017. https://www.fastcompany.com/3067188/how-and-why-to-master-the-habit-of-delaying-gratification.

Department of Health and Human Services. "Physical Activity Guidelines for Americans, 2nd Edition," 2018. https://health.gov/sites/default/files/2019-09/Physical_Activity_Guidelines_2nd_edition.pdf.

DGA. "Dietary Guidelines for Americans," n.d. https://www.dietaryguidelines.gov/.

Dive. "SMART Goals to Improve Your Time Management Skills," n.d. https://www.letsdive.io/blog/smart-goals-to-improve-your-time-management-skills.

Dorob. "5 Tips to Save Your Posture While Studying from Home." *Algonquin College* (blog), n.d. https://www.algonquincollege.com/contenthub/2020/12/08/5-tips-to-save-your-posture-while-studying-from-home/.

Dubey, Tanvi. "20 Inspirational Quotes for Every Woman Chasing Her Dreams Read More at: Https://Yourstory.Com/Herstory/2019/07/Inspirational-Quotes-Woman-Oprah-Winfrey-Kalpana-Chawla." Her Story, July 28, 2019. https://yourstory.com/herstory/2019/07/inspirational-quotes-woman-oprah-winfrey-kalpana-chawla.

Ejsing, Camilla. "5 Tips for an Ergonomic Study Posture." FLEXA, n.d. https://flexaworld.com/blogs/news/5-tips-for-an-ergonomic-study-posture.

Emily Post. "Proper Table Setting 101." Emily Post Etiquette, n.d. https://emilypost.com/advice/table-setting-guides.

Evolve. "Teen Stress and Anxiety: Facts and Statistics," April 1, 2019. https://evolvetreatment.com/blog/teen-stress-anxiety-facts/.

Fairbank, Rachel. "New Study Strengthens the Link Between Exercise and Memory." *The New York Times*, October 7, 2022, sec. Well. https://www.nytimes.com/2022/10/07/well/move/exercise-memory.html.

Familydoctor.org Editorial Staff. "Vitamins and Minerals: How to Get What You Need." familydoctor.org, October 1, 2007. https://familydoctor.org/vitamins-and-minerals-how-to-get-what-you-need/.

FCCLA. "Family, Career and Community Leaders of America," n.d. https://fcclainc.org/.

Fernandez, Jesse. "12 Ways to Exercise While You Study. You Can Do #7 on the Go." American University of Antigua, September 30, 2014. https://www.auamed.org/blog/12-ways-exercise-study/.

Field, Kelly. "Why Starting Career Education in Middle School Pays Off." The Hechinger Report, November 22, 2022. http://hechingerreport.org/the-path-to-a-career-could-start-in-middle-school/.

Gaynor, Emily. "The Complete Guide to Shaving in the Summer." Teen Vogue, June 22, 2015. https://www.teenvogue.com/story/summer-shaving-tips.

Giang, Vivian. "These Are Long-Term Effects of Multitasking." Fast Company, n.d., March 1, 2016. https://www.fastcompany.com/3057192/these-are-the-long-term-effects-of-multitasking.

Gill, Lisa L. "How to Avoid 7 Hidden Fees." CR: Consumer Reports, February 1, 2024. https://www.consumerreports.org/money/fees-billing/how-to-avoid-hidden-fees-a2447151832/.

Goodreads. "A Quote from Hush, Don't Say Anything to God," n.d. https://www.goodreads.com/quotes/420780-do-you-know-what-you-are-you-are-a-manuscript.

Goodreads. "Soulful Living Quotes (25 Quotes)," n.d. https://www.goodreads.com/quotes/tag/soulful-living.

Green, Mitchell. "The Significance of Self-Expression." ResearchGate, November 2007. https://www.researchgate.net/publication/283393312_The_Significance_of_Self-Expression.

Griffiths, Rachael. "The Best Skin-Care Routine for Teens and Tweens, According to Dermatologists." The Strategist, January 30, 2024. https://nymag.com/strategist/article/best-skincare-routine-for-teens.html.

Guthridge, Liz. "Council Post: Want To Improve? Rewire Your Brain's Neural Pathways." Forbes, n.d. https://www.forbes.com/sites/forbescoachescouncil/2024/01/23/want-to-improve-rewire-your-brains-neural-pathways/.

Hamilton, John. "Multitasking Teens May Be Muddling Their Brains." NPR, October 9, 2008, sec. Your Health. https://www.npr.org/2008/10/09/95524385/multitasking-teens-may-be-muddling-their-brains.

Harvard T.H. Chan: The Nutrition Source. "Stress and Health," October 5, 2020. https://nutritionsource.hsph.harvard.edu/stress-and-health/.

Health.gov. "Dietary Reference Intakes," n.d. https://health.gov/our-work/nutrition-physical-activity/dietary-guidelines/dietary-reference-intakes.

Hebert, Marsha. "Creating a Career Vision Board: A Visual Guide to Your Dream Career." TopResume, n.d. https://www.topresume.com/career-advice/creating-a-career-vision-board-a-visual-guide-to-your-dream-career.

Hong, Hana, and Leah Lopez Cardenas. "How to Measure Your Bra Size at Home." Real Simple, October 4, 2023. https://www.realsimple.com/beauty-fashion/clothing/shopping-guide/how-to-measure-bra-size.

Hughes, Melissa. "The Secret to Rewire a Happier, Smarter Brain." Neuro Nugget, May 27, 2021. https://www.melissahughes.rocks/post/the-secret-to-rewire-a-happier-smarter-brain.

ICDL Arabia: Online Sense. "87 Inspirational Quotes about Bullying," January 18, 2017. https://onlinesense.org/bullying-quotes/.

Impressive Teens. "Top 10 Career Sites for High School Students Revealed!," May 15, 2023. https://www.impressiveteens.com/top-career-sites-for-high-school-students/.

Indeed Editorial Team. "120 Essential Skills To List on a Resume." Indeed, June 30, 2023. https://www.indeed.com/career-advice/career-development/skills-list.

Issa, Mo. "13 Rumi Poems to Awaken the Love Within Us." Medium (blog), July 6, 2017. https://mo-issa.medium.com/13-rumi-poems-to-awaken-the-love-within-us-2fcba19ca1c6.

John Hopkins Medicine. "Healthy Eating During Adolescence," May 21, 2024. https://www.hopkinsmedicine.org/health/wellness-and-prevention/healthy-eating-during-adolescence.

Jubbal, Kevin. "How Exercise Makes You Smarter (And a Better Student!)." Med School Insiders, December 22, 2022. https://medschoolinsiders.com/lifestyle/how-exercise-makes-you-smarter-and-a-better-student/.

Kamkar, Amirreza, and OAE IAU. Milky Way Arch over Lut Desert, Iran, by Amirreza

Kamkar, Iran (Islamic Republic Of). August 25, 2021. https://doi.org/10. 5281/ZENODO.5425799.

Kennedy Shriver, Eunice. "What Causes Normal Puberty, Precocious Puberty, & Delayed Puberty?" NICHD: National Institute of Child Health and Human Development, June 21, 2021. https://www.nichd.nih.gov/health/topics/puberty/conditioninfo/causes.

Khona, Minal. "16 Effective Skin Care Tips For Teenagers." SkinKraft, August 25, 2022. https://skinkraft.com/blogs/articles/skin-care-tips-for-teenagers.

Kijowska, Wiktoria. "Sanitary Suspenders to Mooncups: A Brief History of Menstrual Products." Victoria and Albert Museum, n.d. https://www.vam.ac.uk/articles/a-brief-history-of-menstrual-products.

Kubala, Jillian. "Healthy Eating for Teens: What You Need to Know." Healthline, June 20, 2022. https://www.healthline.com/nutrition/healthy-eating-for-teens.

LaForce, Ali. "Time Management Strategies," n.d. https://staff.uccs.edu/sites/g/files/kjihxj2081/files/inline-files/Time-Management-Strategies.pdf.

Laoyan, Sarah. "Why You Should Eat the Frog First [2024] • Asana." Asana, February 2024. https://asana.com/resources/eat-the-frog.

Laskowski, Edward R. "Sitting Risks: How Harmful Is Too Much Sitting?" Mayo Clinic, n.d. https://www.mayoclinic.org/healthy-lifestyle/adult-health/expert-answers/sitting/faq-20058005.

Lazar, Sara W., Catherine E. Kerr, Rachel H. Wasserman, Jeremy R. Gray, Douglas N. Greve, Michael T. Treadway, Metta McGarvey, et al. "Meditation Experience Is Associated with Increased Cortical Thickness." *Neuroreport* 16, no. 17 (November 28, 2005): 1893–97. https://www.ncbi.nlm.nih.gov/pmc/articles/PMC1361002/.

Learning Center. "Movement and Learning," n.d. https://learningcenter.unc.edu/tips-and-tools/movement-and-learning/.

LifeSpan. "Using a Bike Desk for Weight Loss," May 16, 2022. https://www.lifespanfit ness.com/blogs/news/using-a-bike-desk-for-weight-loss.

Lindner, Jannik. "Must-Know Time Management Statistics [Latest Report]." Gitnux, May 27, 2024. https://gitnux.org/time-management-statistics/.

Lucy V Hay & Lizzie Fry. "7 Exercises You Can Do While Reading A Book (Yes, Really!)," n.d. https://lucyvhayauthor.com/7-exercises-you-can-do-while-reading-a-book-yes-really/.

Lumen College Success. "Identify Your Time Management Style," n.d. https://courses. lumenlearning.com/waymaker-collegesuccess/chapter/text-identify-your-time-management-style/.

Mae, Angela. "Macronutrients: Definition, Importance, and Food Sources." MedicalNewsToday, September 30, 2021. https://www.medicalnewstoday.com/arti cles/what-are-macronutrients.

Marquette. "Effective Time Management for Students and Professionals," January 3, 2024. https://online.marquette.edu/business/blog/effective-time-management-for-students-and-professionals.

Martin, Liam. "What Are the Different Time Management Styles?" Time Doctor Blog, November 2, 2020. https://www.timedoctor.com/blog/time-management-styles/.

MBA Financial Strategists. "What Is Delayed Gratification?" n.d. https://www.mbafs.com.au/in-the-news/latest-articles/how-can-delayed-gratification-help-you-with-your-finances/.

Medal, Andrew. "6 Ways to Train Your Brain to Literally Get Smarter." Inc., October 26, 2016. https://www.inc.com/andrew-medal/6-ways-to-train-your-brain-to-literally-get-smarter.html.

Menon, Amrita. "Louis Braille: The Journey of the Inventor of the Braille System." *Medium* (blog), May 24, 2023. https://medium.com/@menonamrita2/louis-braille-the-journey-of-the-inventor-of-the-braille-system-867fc18ea5c9.

MHA. "Youth Ranking 2023." Mental Health America, n.d. https://mhanational.org/issues/2023/mental-health-america-youth-data.

middleearththnj. "The Reasons Behind Teens' Risky Behavior And What Parents Can Do." Middle Earth, October 13, 2014. https://middleearthnj.org/2014/10/13/the-reasons-behind-teens-risky-behavior-and-what-parents-can-do/.

Miller, Kelly. "What Is Delayed Gratification? 5 Examples & Definition." PositivePsychology.com, December 30, 2019. https://positivepsychology.com/delayed-gratification/.

Naik, Anita. "Financial Milestones for Kids: An Age-by-Age Guide." GoHenry, October 27, 2022. https://www.gohenry.com/us/blog/financial-education/financial-milestones-for-kids-an-age-by-age-guide.

Nall, Rachel. "8 Homemade Face Scrubs for Healthier Skin." Healthline, February 25, 2020. https://www.healthline.com/health/homemade-facial-scrub.

Nance-Nash, Sheryl. "20 Hidden Fees You Had No Idea You Were Paying." *Reader's Digest* (blog), n.d. https://www.rd.com/list/hidden-fees-you-had-no-idea-you-were-paying/.

NCDAS. "Teenage Drug Use Statistics [2023]: Data & Trends on Abuse," n.d. https://drugabusestatistics.org/teen-drug-use/.

New York State. "What Does a Healthy Relationship Look Like?" n.d. https://www.ny.gov/teen-dating-violence-awareness-and-prevention/what-does-healthy-relationship-look.

Newton, H.C. "7 Workouts for Book Lovers to Try." *The Irresponsible Reader* (blog), May 19, 2022. https://irresponsiblereader.com/2022/05/19/7-workouts-for-book-lovers-to-try/.

NHS: National Health Service. "Sitting Exercises," January 26, 2022. https://www.nhs.uk/live-well/exercise/sitting-exercises/.

NIH News in Health. "Practicing Gratitude," February 28, 2019. https://newsinhealth.nih.gov/2019/03/practicing-gratitude.

NIMH. "Any Anxiety Disorder." National Institute of Mental Health, n.d. https://www.nimh.nih.gov/health/statistics/any-anxiety-disorder.

Nottingham Trent University. "Poetry Is Good for Mental Health, Study Shows," n.d. https://www.ntu.ac.uk/about-us/news/news-articles/2023/11/poetry-is-good-for-mental-health,-study-shows.

O'Connor, Anahad. "It's Not Just What You Eat, but the Time of Day You Eat It."

*Washington Post*, January 11, 2023. https://www.washingtonpost.com/wellness/2023/01/10/meal-timing-big-meals/.

Olsson, Regan. "10 Things Every Teen Should Know About Skin Care." Banner Health, May 16, 2022. https://www.bannerhealth.com/healthcareblog/better-me/dermatologist-recommended-skin-care-tips-for-teens-and-young-adults.

Oppland, Mike. "13 Most Popular Gratitude Exercises & Activities." PositivePsychology, April 28, 2017. https://positivepsychology.com/gratitude-exercises/.

Page, Amber. "Exercising before Study: The Benefits." Jamworks, December 26, 2022. https://jamworks.com/news/exercising-before-study/.

Palmer, Angela. "11 Tips for Treating Acne in Teenagers." Verywell Health, March 12, 2024. https://www.verywellhealth.com/treating-teen-acne-in-boys-15939.

Parade. "101 Best Friend Quotes To Send Your BFF." Parade, March 4, 2024. https://parade.com/947443/parade/best-friend-quotes/.

Patel, Neil. "When, How, and How Often to Take a Break." Inc., December 11, 2014. https://www.inc.com/neil-patel/when-how-and-how-often-to-take-a-break.html.

Paulus, Nathan. "Teens' Guide to Building a Strong Personal Finance Foundation." MoneyGeek, February 16, 2022. https://www.moneygeek.com/financial-planning/personal-finance-for-teens/.

Pels, Salley, and Emily Allen. "Menstruation and Teenagers - All About Periods." Lifespan, April 1, 2021. https://www.lifespan.org/lifespan-living/menstruation-and-teenagers-all-about-periods.

Perry, Elizabeth. "What Is Networking and Why Is It So Important? (Plus Tips)," May 15, 2023. https://www.betterup.com/blog/networking.

Pulapaka, Shilpa. "Self Development through Reflective Practice." *Medium* (blog), April 6, 2023. https://medium.com/@shilpa.ukau/self-development-through-reflective-practice-75cd36bbd2ff.

RAINN. "Tips for Safer Online Dating and Dating App Use | RAINN," n.d. https://www.rainn.org/articles/tips-safer-online-dating-and-dating-app-use.

Ramanathan, Tom Gurin, Surya. "Career Exploration Activities for High School Students." Polygence, May 20, 2024. https://www.polygence.org/blog/career-exploration-activities-for-students.

Rao, T. J. "The Path to Purpose: What I Learned About Life From Confucius." *Medium* (blog), March 10, 2021. https://tejasraoblog.medium.com/the-path-to-purpose-what-i-learned-about-life-from-confucius-296c4acef302.

Rape Crisis England & Wales. "What Is Sexual Consent?" n.d. https://rapecrisis.org.uk/get-informed/about-sexual-violence/sexual-consent/.

Rockwell Razors. "A Beginner's Guide To Shaving For Young Women," September 15, 2022. https://getrockwell.com/blogs/blogs-about-shaving/a-beginners-guide-to-shaving-for-young-women.

Ryder, Gina. "How to Rewire Your Brain to Change Old Patterns." Psych Central, November 12, 2021. https://psychcentral.com/health/what-is-neuroplasticity.

SAOTG: Staying Ahead of the Game. "How Posture Affects Learning," n.d. https://saotg.com/how-posture-affects-learning/.

Scott, Elizabeth. "Power Napping for Productivity, Stress Relief and Health." Verywell Mind, October 22, 2023. https://www.verywellmind.com/power-napping-health-benefits-and-tips-stress-3144702.

Sharkey, Sarah. "Financial Literacy For Teenagers: Key Money Tips For Teens." Clever Girl Finance, May 3, 2022. https://www.clevergirlfinance.com/financial-literacy-for-teenagers/.

Shetty, Maya. "Optimism as a Means to a Longer Life | Gratitude & Reflection." Lifestyle Medicine, November 14, 2023. https://longevity.stanford.edu/lifestyle/2023/11/14/optimism-as-a-means-to-a-longer-life/.

Stanford Medicine Children's Health. "Exercise and Teenagers," n.d. https://www.stanfordchildrens.org/en/topic/default?id=exercise-and-teenagers-90-P01602.

Strauss, Ilene. "The Benefits of Delaying Gratification." Psychology Today, December 26, 2017. https://www.psychologytoday.com/us/blog/your-emotional-meter/201712/the-benefits-delaying-gratification.

Tarkkanen, Ahti. "Blindness of Johann Sebastian Bach." *Acta Ophthalmologica* 91, no. 2 (March 2013): 191–92. https://doi.org/10.1111/j.1755-3768.2011.02366.x.

Team KT. "The History of Periods | Medieval to Modern Menstruation." Kt. by Knix for Your Teen, May 23, 2018. https://www.knixteen.com/blogs/the-rag/the-history-of-periods.

Teenage Survival Coach. "CRASH - A Is for Accountability," n.d. http://43.250.140.32/~shbrewer/teenagesurvivalcoach.com/crash-program-dashboard/crash-a-is-for-accountability/.

Teenology. "Top Hair Care Tips for Teenagers & Young Adults," June 18, 2021. https://teenology.com/blogs/news/hair-care-tips-for-teens-young-adults.

Texas OnCourse. "Essential Workplace Skills," April 9, 2021. https://blog.texasoncourse.org/educator/essential-workplace-skills.

Texas OnCourse. "The Basics of Career Exploration for Students," June 3, 2021. https://blog.texasoncourse.org/educator/the-basics-of-career-exploration-for-students.

The Learning Network. "Is It Actually Smart to Sit Still?" *The New York Times*, May 31, 2018, sec. The Learning Network. https://www.nytimes.com/2018/05/31/learning/is-it-actually-smart-to-sit-still.html.

The Times of India. "These Rumi Quotes Power Self Worth," September 25, 2016. https://toistudent.timesofindia.indiatimes.com/news/omg/these-rumi-quotes-power-self-worth/8078.html.

TODAY Parenting Team. "Debunking the Belief That Sitting Equals Learning," November 7, 2016. http://community.today.com/parentingteam/post/debunking-the-belief-that-sitting-equals-learning.

U.S. Bureau of Labor Statistics. "K-12: Career Exploration," n.d. https://www.bls.gov/k12/students/careers/career-exploration.htm.

Odendahl, Sarah. University of Minnesota Extension. "Youth Activity: Manage Your Time for Well-Being," 2023. n.d. https://extension.umn.edu/youth-learning-and-skills/daily-time-management-wellbeing.

WebMD Editorial Contributors. "Are There Health Benefits to Drinking Infused

Water?" WebMD, September 13, 2022. https://www.webmd.com/diet/health-bene fits-infused-water.

WebMD Editorial Contributors. "Shaving Tips for Teen Girls." WebMD, December 7, 2022. https://www.webmd.com/teens/shaving-tips-girls.

Women Who Money. "10 Essential Financial Literacy Tips for Teens | Medi-Share." Medi-Share, https://www.medishare.com/blog/10-essential-money-lessons-every-teen-should-learn. https://www.medishare.com/blog/10-financial-literacy-tips-for-teens.

World Health Organization. "Micronutrients," n.d. https://www.who.int/health-topics/micronutrients.

X (formerly Twitter). "Being Independent Means Writing One's Own Story Every Day.," October 8, 2016. https://x.com/om/status/784830601803227136.

Youth.gov. "Career Exploration and Skill Development," n.d. https://youth.gov/youth-topics/youth-employment/career-exploration-and-skill-development.

ZABRISKIE, HANNAH A., and EDWARD M. HEATH. "Effectiveness of Studying When Coupled with Exercise-Induced Arousal." *International Journal of Exercise Science* 12, no. 5 (August 1, 2019): 979–88. https://www.ncbi.nlm.nih.gov/pmc/articles/PMC6719811/.

Zuperly. "LEARN, UNLEARN & RELEARN." *Medium* (blog), August 11, 2021. https://gozuperly.medium.com/alwin-toffler-argued-that-the-illiterate-of-the-21st-century-will-not-be-those-who-cannot-read-and-941aa0bcd55b.

Made in the USA
Columbia, SC
28 December 2024

50761174R00091